Learning for Life and Wor
Home Economics
For NI Key Stage 3

Nicola Anderson
Sharon McKee

Hodder Murray
A MEMBER OF THE HODDER HEADLINE GROUP

The Publishers would like to thank the following for permission to reproduce copyright material:

Photo credits
p.6 Rosenfeld/Mauritius Die Bildagentur Gmbh/Photolibrary Group; **p.7** *top to bottom* © iStockphoto.com/Joey Nelson, © iStockphoto.com/Andriy Doriy, www.purestockX.com, www.purestockX.com, © iStockphoto.com/Michael Valdez; **p.8** © IMAGEiN/Alamy; **p.9** *t* © Food Alan King/Alamy, *b* © geogphotos/Alamy; **p.10** © Neil Holmes Freelance Digital/Alamy; **p.11** *t* Food Standards Agency (FSA), *b* Sainsbury's; **p.12** © Tim Pannell/Corbis; **p.14** © Tim Garcha/zefa/Corbis; **p.16** Nicola Anderson; **p.18** *l* © Food Features/Alamy, *r* Victoria Pearson/FoodPix/Jupiter Images; **p.20** British Heart Foundation; **p.21** *t* Erik Dreyer/Taxi/Getty Images, *l*, *tr* & *br* www.purestockX.com; **p.30** © Liu Liqun/Corbis; **p.35** Paul Poplis/FoodPix/Jupiter Images; **p.38** © Ariel Skelley/Corbis; **p.42** © Heiko Wolfraum/dpa/Corbis; **p.44** © Mark M. Lawrence/Corbis; **p.46** *safe*food; **p.51** *l* Steve Meddle/Rex Features, *r* © Rob Wilkinson/Alamy; **p.53** Eaglemoss/Photolibrary.com; **p.54** © Jim Craigmyle/Corbis; **p.55** Elea Dumas/Nonstock/Jupiter Images; **p.57** © Jim Wileman/Alamy; **p.58** © Rebecca Emery/Corbis; **p.63** © Janine Wiedel Photolibrary/Alamy; **p.64** Diane Bondareff/AP Photo/Empics; **p.66** *A* © Ian Shaw/Alamy, *B* © Enigma/Alamy, *C* © Sandii McDonald/Alamy, *D* © Dennis MacDonald/Alamy; **p.68** © Poppy Berry/zefa/Corbis; **p.69** Nicola Anderson; **p.74** www.purestockX.com; **p.77** © imagebroker/Alamy; **p.80** the FAIRTRADE mark is a Certification Mark and a registered trademark of Fairtrade Labelling Organisations International (FLO) of which the Fairtrade Foundation is a member; **p.84** © David J. Green/Alamy; **p.86** *t* MasterCard Worldwide, *b* © Andrew Paterson/Alamy; **p.87** APACS; **p.92** *t* Citizens Advice, *ct* Consumer Council, *cb* Department of Enterprise, Trade and Investment, *b* Which?; **p.93** BBC.

Text Acknowledgements
p.7 Leaflet text with permission of the Health Promotion Agency; **p.20** poster reproduced courtesy of the British Heart Foundation; **p.33** Tesco Stores Ltd.; **p.64** 'My Top Ten Rules' reproduced by permission of Hodder and Stoughton Limited; **p.89** & **92** the Consumer Council for Northern Ireland and Consumerline.

Every effort has been made to trace all copyright holders, but if any have been inadvertently overlooked the Publishers will be pleased to make the necessary arrangements at the first opportunity.

Although every effort has been made to ensure that website addresses are correct at time of going to press, Hodder Murray cannot be held responsible for the content of any website mentioned in this book. It is sometimes possible to find a relocated web page by typing in the address of the home page for a website in the URL window of your browser.

Hodder Headline's policy is to use papers that are natural, renewable and recyclable products and made from wood grown in sustainable forests. The logging and manufacturing processes are expected to conform to the environmental regulations of the country of origin.

Orders: please contact Bookpoint Ltd, 130 Milton Park, Abingdon, Oxon OX14 4SB. Telephone: (44) 01235 827720. Fax: (44) 01235 400454. Lines are open 9.00–5.00, Monday to Saturday, with a 24-hour message answering service. Visit our website at www.hoddereducation.co.uk

© Nicola Anderson and Sharon McKee 2007
First published in 2007 by
Hodder Murray, an imprint of Hodder Education,
a member of the Hodder Headline Group
an Hachette Livre UK company,
338 Euston Road
London NW1 3BH

Impression number   5 4 3 2
Year   2011 2010 2009 2008 2007

Cover photos: *Parents with baby*, © Kayoco/zefa/Corbis; *Shopping cart with food*, © imagebroker/Alamy; *Computer screen detail* 'Buy' button, © Andrew Paterson/Alamy.
Illustrations by Oxford Designers and Illustrators
Designed in 10.5/14pt ITC Stone Serif by Janet McCallum
Printed in Italy

A catalogue record for this title is available from the British Library

ISBN-13: 978 0340 927 113

CONTENTS

INTRODUCTION

Home Economics is one strand of Learning for Life and Work. It is a subject through which many skills can be developed, in particular the practical skills involved in planning, preparing, cooking and serving food.

This book has been created to form part of the Key Stage 3 Home Economics experience and does not have to be followed in chapter order. It is divided into three sections.

SECTION 1: HEALTHY EATING

Within this section of the book you will have opportunities to learn about healthy food choices, nutrition, the consequences of poor food choices, how to prevent food poisoning, how religion affects what we eat, and food packaging and labelling.

SECTION 2: HOME AND FAMILY LIFE

Within this section of the book you will have opportunities to learn about family life and the nutritional needs of a range of family members. There is also an A–Z of surviving adolescence and information on how to cope with different family circumstances.

SECTION 3: INDEPENDENT LIVING

Within this section of the book you will have opportunities to learn about how you can be an ethical consumer, shopping online, how to pay for what you buy, your rights as a consumer and organisations out there to help you with consumer issues.

FEATURES OF THE BOOK

In each chapter you will find:

- **Learning intentions**
Each chapter starts by outlining the learning intentions – these are the skills and knowledge you should be learning as you make your way through the chapter.

- **Activities**

Each chapter has a number of activities. You may be asked to work as an individual, in pairs, in small groups or as a class. The activities work best when you are enthusiastic, give them a go and develop and agree some helpful ground rules for working with others.

- **Glossary words**

These appear in small capitals and are defined in the Glossary at the end of the book.

- **Thinking skills and personal capabilities**

Alongside each activity there is an icon. There are five different icons in all and these highlight the main thinking skills and personal capabilities you will be developing while carrying out the activity. The table below shows which skills each icon stands for.

Skill	Icon	Description
Managing Information		Research and manage information effectively to investigate personal development, citizenship and employability issues.
Thinking, Problem Solving, Decision Making		Show deeper understanding by thinking critically and flexibly, solving problems and making informed decisions.
Being Creative		Demonstrate creativity and initiative when developing ideas and following them through.
Working with Others		Work effectively with others.
Self-Management		Demonstrate self-management by working systematically, persisting with tasks, evaluating and improving own performance.

<table>
</table>

Learning intentions

I am learning:

✓ what the BALANCE OF GOOD HEALTH is
✓ the importance of each of the five food groups within the Balance of Good Health.

WHAT IS THE BALANCE OF GOOD HEALTH?

The Balance of Good Health is a commonly used way of dividing foods into five food groups. The five food groups are:

- fruit and vegetables
- bread, cereal and potatoes
- meat, fish and alternatives
- milk and dairy foods
- fatty and sugary foods.

A BALANCED DIET will consist of a range of foods from each of the five food groups in the correct proportions, as the photo below shows. A balanced diet is not always achieved in each meal but should be achieved over several days or a week. No single food can provide the body with all the NUTRIENTS it needs, so it is essential that a wide variety of different foods are eaten regularly.

The Balance of Good Health

Activity 1

a) With a partner, draw up a list of six questions and answers about the Balance of Good Health. Give the six answers you have come up with to another pair. They then must think of a question that could match each answer. Are they the same as the questions you came up with?

b) Feedback to the class what you have learned about the Balance of Good Health.

Fruits and vegetables

There are many varieties of fruits and vegetables and we can enjoy them fresh, frozen, dried, canned or as part of a drink. Fruits and vegetables contain a wide range of the essential nutrients and are important in fighting disease and for overall good health. They provide good sources of FIBRE to help keep the digestive system healthy. We are advised to eat five portions of a variety of fruits and vegetables each day.

PORTIONS FOR EXTRA HEALTH

In Northern Ireland we eat on average 3 portions of fruit and veg a day. Health experts recommend at least 5 portions each day – so most of us need to eat more! Remember that frozen, canned and dried fruit and veg count as well.

As a guide, each of the following counts as 1 portion:
- 1 slice of large fruit, e.g. melon or pineapple;
- 1 piece of medium sized fruit, e.g. a pear or a banana;
- 2 small fruit, e.g. kiwis, mandarins or plums;
- 1 cup of very small fruit, e.g. grapes or strawberries;
- 1 glass of fruit juice (fruit juice can only be counted as 1 portion of the 5 each day);
- 2–3 heaped tablespoons of vegetables;
- 1 dessert bowl of salad.

We usually think of potatoes as vegetables, but they are starchy foods, like rice and bread. They're not counted in our 5 portions, but we should still eat them for the fibre they contain.

A piece of fruit makes a good snack at any time of day. By eating one extra portion of fruit or vegetables every day, it's easy to build up to the recommended 5 a day.

A leaflet from the Health Promotion Agency entitled *100% pure five. Five a day – the healthy way.*

 ## Activity 2

Look at the leaflet above. It explains what makes a portion of fruit and vegetables.

a) Carry out a class survey to find out how many portions of fruit and vegetables pupils in your class eat in a typical day. You could present your findings as a bar chart.

b) Analyse what you have found out. How might young people's eating habits affect their overall health now and in the future?

 ## Activity 3

Your canteen is promoting healthy eating through encouraging teenagers to eat more fruit and vegetables. Design a tray mat that will promote this healthy eating message to teenagers eating in your canteen.

REVIEW

a) Examine three of the completed tray mats from Activity 3. For each mat write down two things you like and suggest one way you think the design could be improved.

b) Read through and think about the comments made about your tray mat by other pupils. Use their comments to write a short evaluation on how you could improve your tray mat.

Bread, cereals and potatoes

Foods in this group are important for providing us with energy and fibre. Foods in this group include pasta, rice, noodles, different varieties of bread and potatoes.

Bread is a good source of energy and fibre.

 ## Activity 4

a) As a class, make a list of as many types of bread as you can think of. Remember to include a wide variety both from Northern Ireland and from other countries around the world. You could visit a bakery or supermarket or research using a supermarket website.

b) Choose one type of bread and write a short fact file. You could include:
   - which part of the world the bread comes from originally
   - ingredients
   - how it is made
   - how it is served
   - how it contributes to a balanced diet
   - how much it would cost to buy.

c) Use a basic bread recipe and modify it to create a different variety of bread that you would enjoy eating - for example, cinnamon bread, cheese bread, or apple and raisin bread.

Meat, fish and alternatives

Foods in this group are good SOURCES of PROTEIN, which is needed for growth and repair of the body. Foods in this group include beef, lamb, pork, poultry, all varieties of fish, eggs, pulses, nuts and alternatives to meat such as tofu and Quorn.

Meat is a good source of protein.

  ## Activity 5

a) Find out about the range of alternatives to meat. You could do some research using the internet or visit the supermarket. What products are available to use as a substitute for meat? What are some of the advantages and disadvantages of these products?

b) As a class, plan, prepare, cook and serve a range of dishes using meat and MEAT ALTERNATIVES, for example, spaghetti Bolognese, chilli con carne, stew, lasagne or curry. Compare the dishes in terms of cost, taste, texture, appearance and smell.

Milk is a good source of calcium.

Milk and dairy foods

Foods in this group are high in CALCIUM and are good for helping to form and maintain strong bones and teeth. Foods include milk, soya milk, yoghurt and cheese.

Many yoghurts and yoghurt drinks use the words 'Live' or 'Bio' on their label. This makes the product appear to be more 'healthy' but in reality it means very little. A more recent development is to advertise yoghurts and yoghurt drinks as containing 'good BACTERIA' and these products often have the word 'PROBIOTIC' on their label. Some research has shown that they may help to promote a healthy digestive system and improve the IMMUNE SYSTEM. However, more research is needed to prove this.

Fatty and sugary foods

Foods from this group include butter, margarine, oils, cream, biscuits, cakes, sweets and sugary drinks. We are encouraged to reduce the amount of fatty and sugary foods that we eat. Eating too much of these foods can lead to health problems such as OBESITY, CORONARY HEART DISEASE, dental decay and type 2 DIABETES. There are many alternative low-fat and low-sugar products available and we should choose carefully in order to reduce our intake of fat and sugar. Many products claim to be 'low fat', 'fat free', 'sugar free' or having 'no added sugar'.

Sweets are high in sugar.

TRAFFIC LIGHT LABELLING

The Food Standards Agency has produced guidelines for MANUFACTURERS to follow regarding the claims they make about their food. They recommend that manufacturers should show the fat, sugar and salt content of food products by using traffic light colours on the packaging. They think this will help CONSUMERS make informed choices about what food they buy. With traffic light colours, consumers can see at a glance if the food they are looking at has high, medium or low amounts of fat, sugar and salt in 100 g of the food. The diagram opposite is an example of one design being used on food packaging.

LOW FAT	LOW SAT FAT	HIGH SUGARS	MED SALT
7.7g Per serve	**2.0g** Per serve	**42.2g** Per serve	**2.0g** Per serve

LOW	**FAT** 7.7g per serving
LOW	**SATURATES** 2.0g per serving
HIGH	**SUGARS** 42.2g per serving
MED	**SALT** 2.0g per serving

A red light on the front of the pack means that the food is high in something we should be trying to cut down on, such as fat, sugar and salt.

An amber light means that the food isn't high or low in fat, sugar and salt, so it is OK to choose this food most of the time.

Green means the food is low in fat, sugar and salt. The more green lights a food has, the healthier the choice.

This label uses the traffic light system recommended by the Food Standards Agency.

This food label shows a traffic light labelling system that Sainsbury's uses.

...Look out for me!

cal 431 | fat 6.8g | sat fat 2.8g | salt 2.0g | total sugars 6g

Activity 6

Some supermarkets have come up with their own design using the traffic light colours. An example is shown above. Look at the traffic light labelling systems the Food Standards Agency and Sainsbury's have come up with. Can you do better?

Design your own easy-to-use system that shows people which foods contain high levels of fat, sugar and salt and which are the healthier choices.

REVIEW

To help you to reflect on what you have learned in this chapter, complete the following sentences:

a) Three things I learned through this chapter are ...

b) Two things I enjoyed about this chapter are ...

c) One thing I would still like to find out about is ...

Learning intentions

I am learning:

- ✓ the FUNCTIONS and sources of the main nutrients
- ✓ how a DEFICIENCY or excess of the main nutrients can cause health problems
- ✓ to work with others in taking turns, sharing and co-operating in a task.

Food is fuel for the body and is necessary to keep us alive and healthy. Without food we cannot survive. All food provides us with nutrients: protein, CARBOHYDRATES, VITAMINS and MINERALS. Each nutrient has a different and important function in the body and our health will suffer if nutrients are not supplied in sufficient amounts. The tables on the opposite page show which foods contain the essential nutrients we need for good health. Most foods contain more than one nutrient and, as we have seen in Chapter 1, in order to ensure we have a balanced diet we should eat a variety of foods. As well as nutrients, the body also needs dietary fibre and water to be healthy.

DIETARY FIBRE

Dietary fibre describes a number of different substances that are not digested but are important to help remove waste from the body. A lack of dietary fibre can result in constipation or bowel disorders. Good sources of dietary fibre include wholegrain breakfast cereals, wholemeal bread, wholemeal pasta, and skins of fruits and vegetables.

WATER

Water is vital for life as 70 per cent of the human body is made up from it. Water is needed for all body fluids such as blood, digestive juices, saliva and urine. Water is also needed to control body temperature and to prevent DEHYDRATION. Many foods such as fruits and vegetables contain water.

Extra water is needed during physical activity.

REVIEW

Create a concept map on the topic of nutrients. Use pictures, words and colour to make your own concept map to help you remember the important points included in this chapter.

 Activity 1

In small teams use the information in this chapter to create five quiz questions to test the other teams' knowledge of nutrients. Think of a team name that is related to this chapter. You will need to select a quizmaster to read out the question when it is your team's turn. You should also choose a scorekeeper to keep score of the answers you get correct. Have fun!

MAJOR NUTRIENTS

Nutrient	Function	Sources	Deficiency\Excess
Carbohydrate	An important source of energy.	Pasta, Bread, Potatoes, Rice } Sugars, Sugary drinks, Sweets, Cakes, Biscuits }	• If more carbohydrate is eaten than required the excess is stored as fat in the body. • Too much sugar can result in type 2 diabetes and/or dental decay.
Protein	• Needed for growth, repair and maintenance of the body. • Excess protein also provides energy.	Meat, Fish, Eggs, Dairy foods, Cereals, Nuts, Peas, Beans, Lentils	A deficiency can lead to KWASHIORKOR. This is rare in Northern Ireland but can occur in developing countries and causes symptoms associated with famine.
Fat	• A concentrated source of energy. • Keeps the body warm. • Protects vital organs and the skeleton. • Provides a source of fat-soluble vitamins.	Meat, Butter, Margarine, Cooking oils, Eggs, Fried foods, Prepared foods such as cakes and biscuits	Too much fat can lead to health problems such as coronary heart disease and obesity.

Vitamins

A	• Essential for night vision. • Needed to promote healthy skin. • Boosts immunity. • Is an ANTI-OXIDANT.	Liver, Dairy foods, Fish, Red and orange fruits and vegetables such as carrots, peppers, apricot and mango	Deficiency can lead to: • night blindness • dry, flaky skin • frequent infections.
B	There are at least thirteen B group vitamins and their main function is to help the body make energy from the food we eat.	Meat, Milk, FORTIFIED breakfast cereals, Eggs, Wholegrain cereals	Deficiency diseases include: • BERI-BERI • PELLAGRA • failure to grow • depression • anaemia.
C	• Needed to make collagen, which holds body cells together. • Helps with the absorption of iron into the bloodstream. • Is an anti-oxidant.	Fruits and vegetables, in particular blackcurrants, kiwi, oranges, strawberries, lemons, green peppers and broccoli	Deficiency can lead to: • SCURVY.
D	Works with calcium to help form strong bones and teeth.	Sunlight, Oily fish, Margarine, Eggs, Cheese	Deficiency can lead to: • RICKETS in children • OSTEOMALACIA in adults.

Minerals

Calcium	• Vital for strong bones and teeth. • Needed for blood clotting and for the functioning of muscles and nerves.	Dairy foods, Green leafy vegetables, Sardines, Dried figs	Deficiency leads to: • poorly formed bones and teeth in children • OSTEOPOROSIS in adults.
Iron	Forms haemoglobin, which is responsible for carrying oxygen around the body.	Meat, Fortified breakfast cereals, Liver, Dried fruits, Green leafy vegetables	Deficiency leads to: • ANAEMIA.
Fluoride	• Helps to harden tooth enamel to make it more resistant to decay. • Strengthens bones.	Tap water, Tea, Seafood, Fluoride toothpaste	Excess can result in mottling of the teeth (dark brown spots).

Learning intentions

I am learning:

✓ about diet-related disorders
✓ the causes of these disorders and how to manage them effectively
✓ to work with others to develop health promotion materials and to review the effectiveness of this work.

This man is obese.

 Activity 1

With a partner, study the photo of the man above. Discuss what health problems he might have and why he might be in this condition.

Some people suffer from health problems that are the result of what they eat. These problems are known as diet-related disorders. Some are the result of consuming too much of a nutrient while others are due to lack of a nutrient. However, for some diet-related disorders, there are many other factors that can contribute to the condition including lack of exercise, smoking, excess alcohol consumption and family history.

OBESITY

The man in the photograph has a condition called obesity, which means that he is at least 20 per cent over the ideal weight for his height and build. In Northern Ireland the number of obese people is increasing. If the current trend continues, by 2010 it is predicted that 23 per cent of women and 22 per cent of men will be obese. The Government has set targets to reduce levels of obesity because it is a cause of premature death and a huge cost to the economy. The health problems linked to obesity can result in people having to take more time off work and needing more health care than a person who is within the normal weight range.

Although obesity can in some cases be due to an imbalance in HORMONES, it is usually caused by overeating and not burning off excess calories through physical activity. The excess calories then convert to fat and are stored in the body, resulting in weight gain and eventually obesity.

There are many health problems related to being obese. An obese person is more at risk of:
• heart disease
• diabetes
• hypertension (high blood pressure)
• chest infections
• varicose veins
• gall stones
• psychological problems such as depression and low self esteem.

CORONARY HEART DISEASE

Coronary heart disease can occur when the small arteries that supply blood to the heart become blocked by a build-up of fatty deposits. This causes the opening in the arteries to narrow and is called atherosclerosis.

When the arteries become partially or totally blocked, the heart has to work much harder to pump blood around the body. If the arteries become totally blocked blood cannot flow to the heart and this can result in a heart attack.

A healthy diet plays a vital role in reducing the risk of coronary heart disease. However, there are many other factors that increase the risk such as a lack of exercise, stress, smoking, high alcohol consumption, high blood pressure and being overweight.

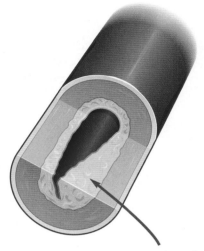

Fatty deposits cause narrowing of the artery.

Reduce SATURATED fat

Replace saturated fats with POLYUNSATURATED fats

Cut off visible fat on meat

Steam, microwave, grill or bake food instead of frying

Be heart smart!

Buy low fat foods

Eat more fruit and vegetables – aim for five a day

Eat more fibre-rich foods to reduce CHOLESTEROL

Be aware of fat you can't see in snack foods, biscuits and cakes

A local university recently published findings from a survey that studied coronary heart disease risk among the young people of Northern Ireland (see the newspaper headline on the right).

 Activity 2

In response to this survey:
a) Design an advice leaflet or poster particularly aimed at the young people in your school on the theme of preventing heart disease. Use 'Be heart smart!' above to help you.
b) Compare your leaflet or poster with others in your class. Which leaflet or poster is most effective in getting the message across? Why?
c) How could you improve your work to make it more effective?

SUNDAY COURIER
By the age of 15, 1 in 4 young people in Northern Ireland is heading for a heart attack

This child has type 1 diabetes and injects insulin twice a day.

 Activity 3

Look at the list of foods and drinks below and suggest low-sugar or sugar-free alternatives that a diabetic could include in their diet. One example has been done for you.

DIABETES

Diabetes is a condition in which the body's normal way of breaking down sugar is not functioning properly. This means the pancreas is not producing any insulin, or not enough insulin, to regulate the amount of sugar (glucose) in the blood. There are two types of diabetes.

Type 1 Diabetes

Type 1 diabetes occurs when the body is unable to produce any insulin. This type of diabetes is most likely to develop before the age of 40. It is controlled with insulin injections, a balanced diet and regular physical activity. Someone with well-controlled diabetes can lead a perfectly normal, active life.

Type 2 Diabetes

Type 2 diabetes occurs when the body makes some insulin but not enough. This type of diabetes usually occurs in people over the age of 40, although more children are now developing the condition. Type 2 diabetes can often be linked to being overweight. It is controlled by lifestyle changes including diet, weight loss and exercise. Treatment may also include taking tablets and having insulin injections.

A person who has diabetes is called a diabetic. Diabetics should be able to enjoy a balanced diet. However, they need to be especially careful about the amount of sugar in their diet in order to help to maintain normal blood sugar levels.

High-sugar foods		→	Low-sugar/sugar-free alternatives
Tinned fruit in syrup		→	Tinned fruit in natural juice
Chocolate biscuits, cakes, pastries		→	
Sugar-coated breakfast cereals		→	
Fruit yoghurts		→	
Jam, marmalade, honey		→	
Sweet puddings, desserts		→	
Sweet, fizzy soft drinks		→	
Sweets, chocolate		→	

Dieticians, whose job it is to work out suitable diets for people with diabetes, do not recommend the use of special diabetic products. These can be expensive and do not necessarily help control diabetes. Making sensible choices about food is what is important.

 Activity 4

Choosing soft drinks can be very confusing for someone with diabetes, as terms such as 'low sugar', 'reduced sugar', 'no added sugar' and 'sugar free' can often be found on labels. Use the internet to research what these terms really mean (a good starting point is www.food.gov.uk). For example, 'low sugar' means that the drink contains no more than five per cent of sugar per 100 ml.

When checking food labels for sugar content, watch out for the following as they are some of the different names given to the sugar found in food – glucose, sucrose, dextrose, fructose, glucose syrup, invert sugar, malto-dextrin.

TOOTH DECAY

Tooth decay is usually caused by a build-up of plaque. Plaque forms when food, saliva and bacteria build up on the surface of the teeth, giving them a furry feel when we run our tongue around them. Acid is produced when the plaque on teeth comes into contact with sugar and this acid eats into tooth enamel and causes tooth decay.

Children and adolescents are particularly at risk of tooth decay. It is vital to establish good habits in childhood in order to protect dental health in the future.

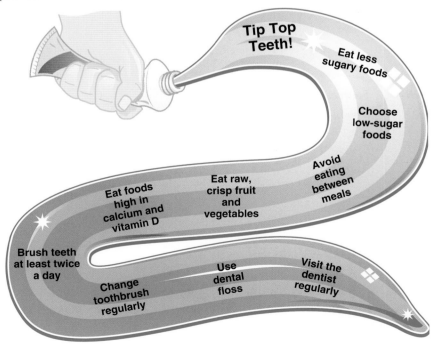

Tip Top Teeth!

Eat less sugary foods

Choose low-sugar foods

Avoid eating between meals

Eat foods high in calcium and vitamin D

Eat raw, crisp fruit and vegetables

Brush teeth at least twice a day

Change toothbrush regularly

Use dental floss

Visit the dentist regularly

 **Activity 5**

a) In groups, design and make a resource that could be used to teach six-year-olds about the importance of looking after their teeth. Use the information on the left to help you.

b) If possible invite a primary school teacher to look at your resources and evaluate how effective they are in getting the message of the importance of dental health across to young children.

ANAEMIA

WHAT'S WRONG WITH ME?

Over the last while people have been telling me that I am really pale. As well as that, I always feel tired and sometimes find it hard to concentrate in school. Just last week during PE I felt really short of breath and had to sit at the side as I thought I was going to faint. What on earth is wrong with me? I'm worried.

Lucy, 14, Newry

It is very likely that Lucy has iron-deficiency anaemia. This is caused by a lack of iron in the body. Iron is essential to form part of a substance called HAEMOGLOBIN, which gives red blood cells their colour. Haemoglobin is needed to carry oxygen around the body to all cells. The symptoms that Lucy describes are exactly those that someone with iron-deficiency anaemia will feel. It is important to consult a doctor for a diagnosis, and treatment will involve increasing the amount of iron-rich foods in the diet. Iron SUPPLEMENTS prescribed by the doctor may also be needed.

Haem iron
This type of iron is in a form that is easily used (absorbed) by the body. It is found in:
Red meat
Liver
Kidney

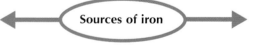
Sources of iron

Non-haem iron
This type of iron is not so easily used by the body and needs vitamin C to help it be absorbed. It is found in:
Fortified breakfast cereals
Dried fruit
Green leafy vegetables
Fortified bread
Pulses

Activity 6

Write a reply to Lucy's letter explaining to her what is wrong with her. Include in your reply advice on how she can make changes to her diet to treat iron-deficiency anaemia.

OSTEOPOROSIS

Osteoporosis is a condition in which the bones become weak and brittle and break easily. It is particularly common in older women after the MENOPAUSE. A good supply of calcium in the diet throughout childhood, adolescence and early adulthood helps to reduce the risk of developing osteoporosis. This is because bones are absorbing calcium and becoming stronger and denser in the early years of life. People's bones are at their strongest when they are aged around 30.

The Dairy Council has highlighted a worrying statistic that in the UK 24 per cent of young people aged 11–14 aren't getting the 800–1000 mg of calcium they need each day. The Council points out that the teenage years are the peak time for building strong bones as the bones are growing at their fastest rate.

As well as eating dairy products each day, weight-bearing exercise such as walking, tennis or aerobics can help to strengthen bones. It is also a good idea to get some sunlight on the skin to build up stores of vitamin D. Vitamin D helps the absorption of calcium from milk and dairy products.

Did you know …

the word 'osteoporosis' is derived from the ancient Greek language and means 'bone that has many holes'.

2 large slices of wholemeal bread = 39 mg of calcium

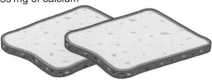

85 g of cooked broccoli = 34 mg of calcium

56 g of dried apricots = 52 mg of calcium

CALCIUM RICH PORTIONS OF FOOD

30 g piece of Cheddar cheese = 216 mg of calcium

200 ml glass of semi-skimmed milk = 248 mg of calcium

150 g pot of low-fat fruit yoghurt = 225 mg of calcium

50g of peanuts = 30 mg of calcium

Activity 7

Are you getting enough?
a) Write a food diary of everything that you eat on a typical day. Use the pictures above to help you estimate how much calcium you get.
- Do you get the recommended 800–1000 mg per day?
- How could you change your diet to increase your calcium intake?
b) Design a day's menu to show a teenager how to include the recommended amount of calcium in their diet. Include a range of calcium-rich foods in your menu.
c) Plan, prepare, cook and serve one of your suggested meals.

REVIEW

Use pictures, words and colour to create a concept map on the topic of diet-related disorders in order to help you remember the important points included in this chapter.

Learning intentions

I am learning:

- ✓ what fast food is and how eating it might affect my health
- ✓ what the most popular types of fast food are in my class
- ✓ to select the most appropriate method to present results
- ✓ to plan, prepare, cook and serve a healthy meal for a child.

 Activity 1

a) Look carefully at the poster below. Discuss it with your class and list the words you would use to describe what you see.

b) Discuss why you think the British Heart Foundation has produced this poster. What message does it give about fast food?

A poster produced by the British Heart Foundation

WHAT IS FAST FOOD?

It's ready to eat as soon as you pay for it.

Burger, chips and fizzy drinks.

Food that you don't have to cook yourself.

Not very healthy but really nice to eat!

 ## Activity 2

a) The teenagers above recognise what fast food is. Use their ideas and the word bank on the right to create your own definition of what fast food is.

b) Most people eat fast food at some time. Why do you think this is? Use the quotes from the teenagers above and the definition you produced to help you answer this question.

Word Bank

simple, **expensive**, *prepared quickly*, tasty, *served*, **fatty**, **cheap**, *healthy*

Did you know ... ?

Many fast food fries are not 100 per cent potato. Up to 20 per cent could be sugar, flour, salt and oil.

Did you know ... ?

Many fast food burgers contain red food colouring to make them look more appealing.

 ## Activity 3

Find out what types of fast food are popular in your class. Consider how you will gather, record and present this information. Select an appropriate way to present your results. You could use ICT to help you record your results and produce a graph.

Did you know ... ?

Some chicken nuggets contain more chicken skin than chicken meat.

FOOD FOR YOUNG CHILDREN

Fast food companies often target young children as they are easily influenced. It is vital that young children develop good food habits as this will determine their diet for life. They must be provided with a balanced diet.

 Activity 4

Many fast food companies produce colourfully packaged meals for children. These often include a drink and a toy as well as the food.

a) Find out what special meals are available for children from your local fast food outlets.

b) Consider one of these meals and evaluate it by completing a table similar to the one below.

Advantages of the meal	Disadvantages of the meal
The child will like it	Could have too much salt in it

  Activity 5

In pairs, develop an idea for a healthier alternative to the meal you evaluated in Activity 4. Plan, prepare, cook and serve your children's meal. Make sure you present it in a way that is fun and tempting for a young child. You may want to include something to encourage children to choose your meal. Use the picture below for some ideas.

 REVIEW

Compare your meal from Activity 5 with others in your class. Think of one way to improve your children's meal.

5 TAKING CARE OF YOUR FOOD

Would You Like Ross to Cook Your Dinner?

Learning intentions

I am learning:

- ✓ to recognise good PERSONAL HYGIENE practices when handling food
- ✓ how to store food correctly
- ✓ how to prevent CONTAMINATION of food during preparation, cooking and serving
- ✓ to collate, record and present information appropriately in an advice leaflet.

🧩 Activity 1

With a partner study the picture of Ross working in his kitchen. It is unlikely that you would want to eat any food prepared by Ross in this kitchen. With your partner decide upon and record ten ways Ross could clean up his act.

PERSONAL HYGIENE

Bacteria that cause food poisoning are easily spread around the kitchen and on to food via hands, cloths, equipment and utensils. It is vital that anyone working with food makes sure that they have a very high standard of personal hygiene and that the kitchen is kept hygienically clean and tidy. This will help to prevent the spread of potentially harmful bacteria.

Long hair should be tied back to reduce the risk of it touching or falling into food. Fact: one hair follicle can contain 500,000 germs!

Always wear a clean apron when preparing food. Do not wipe hands on your apron during food preparation.

All cuts should be covered with a blue plaster.

When preparing food it is also important not to sneeze, spit, smoke or cough over food.

Remove jewellery before preparing food. Fact: there could be as many germs under a ring as there are people in Europe.

Ensure hands are washed thoroughly before and after touching and preparing food.

STORING FOOD CORRECTLY

Food has to be properly stored to ensure that its safety and quality are maintained. There are different storage methods for different foods. Some foods, such as meat and dairy products, are considered high-risk foods and must be stored at the correct temperature in a fridge or freezer, while others, such as dried foods, are considered low risk and will remain safe to eat when stored in a cupboard. It is important to check the BEST BEFORE DATE or USE BY DATE on foods. This information must be printed on any packaging used for food.

Best before end:

JUN 2007

T125854E1545

Best before – this means that the food will be at its best up until this date. Most foods with this type of date mark are low-risk foods and can be stored in a cupboard.

Display until	Use by
21 NOV C	21 NOV 21:40

Use by – this means that food must be eaten by this date. After this date food is likely to become unsafe to eat and could cause food poisoning. Foods with this type of date mark are high-risk foods and should be stored in a fridge or freezer that is operating at the correct temperature to prevent the spread of harmful bacteria.

 Activity 2

In order to help you understand the importance of careful food
storage, match up the following words and their definitions correctly.

a) Fridge

b) Freezer

c) Fruit bowl

d) Cupboard

e) Vegetable rack

1. It is important that this is checked regularly for rotting vegetables.

2. This should be kept clean, well ventilated and dry to ensure food stays fresh.

3. This should operate between 1°C and 5°C and use by dates on foods should be checked regularly.

4. This should operate at –18°C and should not be overloaded. Foods should be labelled and date marked.

5. It is important that this is checked regularly for overripe or mouldy fruit.

Activity 3

Ross is finishing off his weekly shop and must now go home
and store it all correctly in his kitchen. Draw up a table to
record the correct storage area for each item of food in his
trolley. You could then add some more items that are found
in these areas in your kitchen.

PREPARING, COOKING AND SERVING FOOD SAFELY

FOOD POISONING bacteria can multiply and spread when we are handling food. In order to prevent contamination of food, which could cause food poisoning, it is important to prepare, cook, serve and reheat food correctly. The table below outlines some of the rules to follow.

Preparation	Cooking	Serving	Reheating
• Minimise handling of food. • Clean as you go. • Minimise the time that food is in the DANGER ZONE (5–63°C).	• Food should be cooked thoroughly. • The centre of food should reach 70°C.	• Hot food should be served at above 63°C. • Cold food should be served below 5°C.	• Food should not be reheated more than once. • Reheat to 70°C for at least two minutes.

Cross contamination

Cross contamination can occur when bacteria is able to spread from raw foods to foods that are cooked or ready to eat. Chopping boards, knives, utensils, cloths and unwashed hands can all be the cause of cross contamination.

 Activity 4

Look back at the picture of Ross in his kitchen on page 23. Identify examples of how cross contamination could take place as he prepares and cooks his food.

 Activity 5

Use the information from this chapter and carry out additional research to help you produce an advice leaflet for shoppers like Ross on how to store, prepare, cook and serve food safely.

REVIEW

a) Compare your leaflet from Activity 5 with others in your class. Which leaflet is most effective in getting the message across? Why?

b) How could you improve your work to make it more effective?

6 SERIOUSLY SAFE FOOD

Each year it is estimated that as many as 5.5 million people in the UK may suffer from food poisoning – that's one in ten people. The bar chart below shows the numbers of reported food poisoning cases in Northern Ireland between 1985 and 2005.

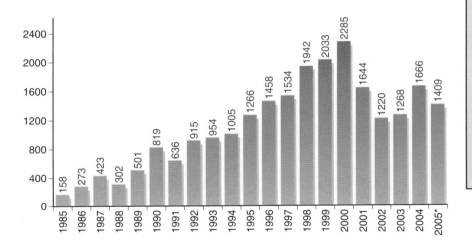

Source: Communicable Disease Surveillance Centre Northern Ireland
* = provisional figures

Notified cases of food poisoning in Northern Ireland, 1985–2005.

 ## Activity 1

Using the data above, answer the following questions:
a) What year had the lowest number of reported cases of food poisoning?
b) What year had the highest number?
c) What has been the trend in the reported cases of food poisoning since 1985?
d) Can you suggest some reasons for the low number of reported cases in the 1980s? Were eating habits different then?
e) Why do you think the number might have risen in the 1990s?
f) The number of reported cases has fallen again in the last five years. Why do you think this might be?
g) Many cases of food poisoning are not reported. Why do you think this is?
h) If you thought you had food poisoning, to whom would you report it?

Fact Box

Food Poisoning

An illness that can occur 1–36 hours after eating contaminated food. Symptoms may include vomiting, diarrhoea, nausea, abdominal pain and fever. There are certain groups of people for whom food poisoning can be very dangerous. They include the very young, the very old, pregnant women and people who are already ill.

Fact Box

Food Hygiene

Good food hygiene ensures that food is safe to eat and that it has been protected from contamination. It also means that potentially harmful bacteria have not been able to multiply, have not caused food spoilage and have been destroyed through cooking.

 **Activity 2**

a) Use the information about the danger zone to create a poster or chart to illustrate the key points about how temperature can affect the growth of harmful food-poisoning bacteria.

b) Evaluate how effective your poster or chart is in getting across the message of the danger zone and how it is linked to food poisoning. Show a family member the poster or chart and get them to explain their understanding of the danger zone.

WHAT CAUSES FOOD POISONING?

The most common cause of food poisoning is bacteria.
- Bacteria can only be seen by using a microscope.
- They are everywhere and are usually harmless.
- They are found in the nose, ears, hair, hands and mouth as well as in cuts and on the skin.
- They are also found in the intestines and can transfer easily if hands are not washed after using the toilet.

How do bacteria grow and survive?

Bacteria grow by splitting in two when the conditions are right. This process is called binary fission. The correct conditions for bacterial growth are moisture, time, food and warmth.

The Danger Zone

The temperature that bacteria like best is around 37°C, which is normal body temperature. As the temperature begins to rise, bacteria find it more difficult to multiply and growth slows down. At temperatures above 63°C bacteria will begin to die. For this reason thorough cooking of food to high temperatures is important.

Bacterial growth also slows down in cold temperatures. In a fridge that is operating at a temperature between 1°C and 5°C, bacteria are dormant or sleepy and will not multiply, although they are not killed. When the food is removed from the fridge and begins to warm up again, bacteria will start to multiply.

If a freezer is operating below -18°C bacteria become dormant or sleepy and will not multiply. However, they are not killed by low temperatures. They are only killed when food is heated to high temperatures.

TYPES OF FOOD POISONING

Name	Sources	Symptoms	Notes
STAPHYLOCOCCUS AUREUS	Foods including cooked meat, pies, custard. Also from the nose, skin, infected cuts and boils.	Severe vomiting and diarrhoea.	Can be transferred to food from hands or from droplets from nose or mouth.
SALMONELLA	Poultry, sausage, eggs, raw meat. Also found in the gut of animals and humans.	Fever, diarrhoea, vomiting and abdominal pain.	It is very likely to cause severe illness in the very young and old.
CLOSTRIDIUM BOTULINUM	Damaged tinned food, especially meat and vegetables.	Double vision, breathing difficulties.	This is a very rare form of food poisoning but can be fatal.
E COLI	Raw and undercooked meats, UNPASTEURISED MILK and dairy foods.	Diarrhoea	Can lead to kidney failure and can sometimes be fatal.
LISTERIA	Soft cheeses, pâté, meat, milk products, prepared salads, COOK-CHILLED foods.	Flu-like symptoms.	Can be very dangerous to pregnant women. Can cause miscarriage and stillbirth.
CAMPYLOBACTER	Raw poultry and meat, unpasteurised milk.	Severe abdominal pain, diarrhoea, fever.	One of the major causes of food poisoning in Northern Ireland.

 Activity 3

Think up an attention-grabbing headline and write a newspaper article that relates to the information covered in this chapter. Your article should inform the general public on various aspects of food safety and the prevention of food poisoning.

REVIEW

In pairs decide together what makes a good newspaper article. Then take turns at reading each other's newspaper article from Activity 3. Tell each other about the strengths of the article and any ways in which you feel it could be improved.

Learning intentions

I am learning:

- ✓ how religion can affect what you eat and how you eat it
- ✓ how to research information and create a fact file about one religion.

 Activity 1

The photograph above shows a Chinese family enjoying a meal. Does this differ from a typical mealtime in your home? If so, in what ways?

People from different cultures often eat different types of foods. A person's culture can include their customs and traditions (the usual way things are done), their way of life and their religion.

Religions often have rules about what can and cannot be eaten.

Did you hear about the new girl called Rebekah in our class? She told us that she is a Jew. Do you know that means that she won't eat some foods?

Well, actually, I knew that Jews don't eat pork but I'm not sure what else – did she tell you?

Well, she said that the Old Testament in the Bible teaches them how to eat and prepare their food. She also said that often her family have a special meal together where they drink a little wine and eat some bread.

Yes, but did she tell you what other foods she is not allowed to eat?

She said that pork, bacon and shellfish are unclean and that their meat must be killed by a special butcher to make it 'kosher'.

What does that mean?

 **Activity 2**

Read Claire and Alison's conversation on page 30.

a) Find out what the term 'kosher' means and write an ending to their conversation.

b) Find out why Jewish people believe that certain foods are unclean. Use the internet for your research. Useful starting points are www.bbc.co.uk/religion and www.reonline.org.uk.

Read what the two teenagers below have to tell you about their religion and how it affects the food they eat.

Hi, my name is Vaneeta and I live in Enniskillen. I am a Hindu. In our religion we believe that the cow is a sacred animal and we treat it with great respect. Therefore cows are not killed for food. Hindus are mainly vegetarian and do not eat beef.

Hi, my name is Mammoon and I live in Belfast. I am a Muslim. We eat most foods but we believe the pig is an unclean animal and will not eat it. Therefore we do not eat any foods containing pork.

Meat is prepared in a special way called HALAL. During RAMADAN, Muslims fast from morning to night – adults eat breakfast before daylight and then fast until sunset.

 Activity 3

a) In pairs, think of five questions you would like to ask Vaneeta, Mammoon or Rebekah to find out more about how their religion affects what they eat.

b) Find out the answers to your questions and write a short fact file about this religion to include information about:
- the special foods that may be eaten during festivals
- foods eaten or not eaten
- preparation and cooking methods
- any other interesting information you find.

You could research your facts using the websites suggested in Activity 2.

REVIEW

Complete the following sentences.

a) In this chapter I learned …

b) I was surprised by …

c) I was especially interested in …

d) One thing I'm not sure about is …

e) The main thing I would like to find out more about is …

f) After this chapter I feel …

WHAT'S ON THE LABEL?

Learning intentions

I am learning:

- ✓ why we need labels on food
- ✓ what information is found on food labels
- ✓ the importance of food packaging
- ✓ to work effectively within a team to adapt a basic recipe
- ✓ skills in the safe, hygienic and creative use of food.

 Activity 1

a) What would help the shopper above make sure he bought baked beans?

b) List three pieces of information he might need to help him decide which can of beans to buy.

WHY DO WE NEED LABELS ON FOOD?

In Activity 1 you may have decided that a food label would help the shopper choose the right product. The main reason for labels is to show us important information about the foods we are eating. This will include the name of the food, how to store it and what the food is made from – the ingredients. Manufacturers also often design labels to ensure they are attractive to us, to tempt us to buy their product.

Shopping for food would be extremely difficult without labels.

What information should be on a food label?

To protect us as consumers the government has set out what information must be on every food label.

Look at the label opposite to see what is required by the Food Labelling Regulations (Northern Ireland) 1996.

Shelf life such as the use by or best before date — **Instructions for use** — **The name of the food** — **Ingredients (in descending order of weight)**

Quantity or weight — **Name and address of the manufacturer** — **Storage instructions**

Activity 2

Using the label above or one you have chosen yourself, make a list of five questions to ask a partner about the information provided on the label.

Other useful information on food labels

Have a look at some information you will often see on a food label.

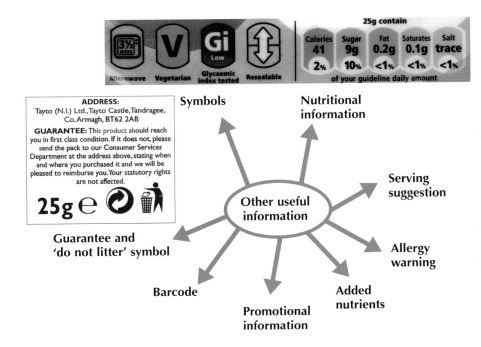

Symbols — **Nutritional information** — **Serving suggestion** — **Allergy warning** — **Added nutrients** — **Promotional information** — **Barcode** — **Guarantee and 'do not litter' symbol**

Other useful information

Activity 3

Collect a range of food labels. In groups examine them closely and create a poster of your own spider diagram, to show the additional information you have found. Find examples of your own for all the useful information, like those shown on the left. Explain why each piece of information is important.

WHAT ABOUT PACKAGING?

 ## Activity 4

Most foods we buy are packaged. Why do you think this is?
Brainstorm at least five reasons.

Now look at the examples of packaging below. Around them are
some reasons why each is used.

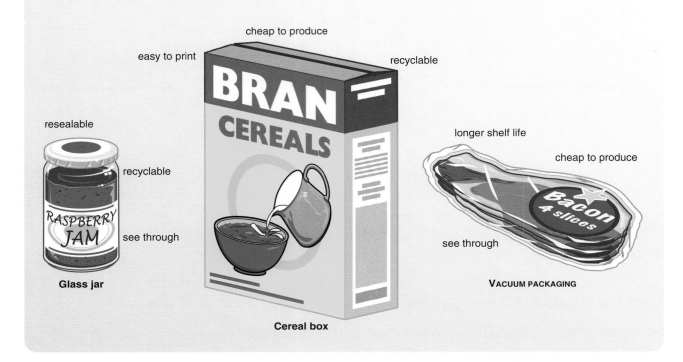

cheap to produce

easy to print

recyclable

resealable

recyclable

longer shelf life

cheap to produce

RASPBERRY JAM

see through

see through

Glass jar

Cereal box

VACUUM PACKAGING

Types of packaging

 ## Activity 5

Copy and complete the table on
the right to show two examples
of how each type of packaging is
used. An example has been done
for you.

Types of packaging	Examples	
Cardboard	Breakfast cereal and some biscuits	
Vacuum packaging		
Tin		
Plastic		
Glass		
Polystyrene		

Muffins

Ingredients (Makes 12 muffins)	Equipment
250 g self-raising flour	Baking bowl
1 teaspoon baking powder	Sieve
100 g caster sugar	Teaspoon
Pinch of salt	Measuring jug
160 ml milk	Two small bowls
100 g melted butter	Muffin cases
2 eggs (beaten)	Muffin tin
100 g selected filling	

Activity 6

The manufacturer of the muffins in the recipe above has asked you to develop a new fruit muffin range aimed at the teenage market.

a) In pairs adapt the recipe above to show an imaginative use of ingredients and design a new product idea.

b) Design the food label for your product, making sure you include all the legal information. Remember you may want to include other useful information that will make your product more appealing to your target market. It may be possible to design your label using ICT.

c) Consider the way your product will be packaged:
- What will be the most suitable type of packaging for your product?
- Could you make your packaging or could you recycle and use empty packets you have at home or in school?

d) Plan, prepare and cook your new product. Remember the health and safety rules of your classroom.

e) Package and label your final product.

f) Ask two other people in your class to taste your new product and give their opinion on it.

REVIEW

Write a detailed evaluation of the work you completed in Activity 6. You could use some of the following questions to help you.

a) How well did you work together with your partner?

b) What have your strengths been?

c) How would you improve your work?

Also take into account the comments made by those who taste-tested your new recipe.

Learning intentions

I am learning:

- ✓ that there is a variety of different family structures
- ✓ how families often share roles and responsibilities
- ✓ that within some families, roles are reversed
- ✓ to develop my own ideas when creating a family instruction manual.

A day in the life of Grace and her family

Another busy day for Grace. She worked a double shift and her daughter Sarah collected her younger brother from the childminder again. It is good that Sarah is able to cook tea for the three of them because Grace often doesn't have time. It's 11p.m. and Sarah is still awake finishing off her homework. She has a lot to do but Year 10 is a difficult year for all young people. Sarah looks tired these days. Matthew is going to his dad's at the weekend so hopefully Sarah and Grace will get a chance to spend some time together. Grace must get some of that ironing done tonight, especially the clean uniforms for tomorrow. Tomorrow is another busy day!

A day in the life of Pete and his family

Pete wasn't sure if he would like his new role in the home but it is turning out to be quite rewarding for him. A typical day has him up at 7.00a.m., busy getting Max fed and changed. Some days he is busy at home with housework and on other days he is out and about – he recently joined a local parent and toddler group. He sometimes misses the company of the men at work but they have been good so far at keeping in touch. It makes sense for him to stay at home now that Max has come along – Judith, his wife, earns more than him so they are saving on childcare. One thing Pete has discovered is that being at home full-time with a baby is hard work and it is sometimes difficult to get everything done before Judith comes home from work in the evening.

 ## Activity 1

Read about each of the families opposite and answer the following questions.
a) What types of family are Grace and Pete part of?
b) What role or roles does each individual have within their family?
c) Make a list of the responsibilities that each individual has within their family.
d) How do Grace's family and Pete's family compare with yours?
e) Write a similar 'a day in the life of ...' that reflects a typical day's routine in your home.

Most people in Northern Ireland live within a family. Our family is an important influence in our lives and makes us who we are. However, no two families are the same. The case studies opposite are examples of a NUCLEAR family and a SINGLE-PARENT FAMILY. There are other family structures in our society including: EXTENDED FAMILY, STEPFAMILY and FOSTER FAMILY.

 ## Activity 2

Think about a television soap that you have watched recently and choose one family featured in the programme, or choose a famous family you know of through the media.
a) What type of family structure do they have?
b) What roles and responsibilities do members of the family have?

ROLES AND RESPONSIBILITIES

Individuals often have a variety of roles within a family, and family members need to be prepared to take on responsibilities to ensure family life is as happy as possible for everyone.

Role reversal

ROLE REVERSAL occurs when traditional roles are exchanged. For example, the man of the house looks after the home and cares for the children while the mother works outside the home and earns money to support the family. This type of role is becoming more common within families in Northern Ireland as women have more career opportunities and work full-time.

Shared roles

It is now very common for both men and women within a family to have full-time jobs. In these circumstances it becomes even more important that all members share the responsibilities of looking after the home and any children within the family. When this occurs family members are said to have SHARED ROLES.

Family mealtimes

A family mealtime.

A newspaper article recently reported that family life is under attack. It suggested that the fall in the number of families who spend time eating meals together is contributing to the breakdown in family life.

Eating meals together as a family gives parents and children the opportunity to talk to each other and find out what has happened during their day. Worries and concerns can be shared and discussed and parents can ensure that their children are eating well and developing good manners.

 ## Activity 3

Plan, prepare, cook and serve a meal that your family could enjoy together.

REVIEW

Take home your completed Family Instruction Manual from Activity 4 and discuss it with an adult. Allow them the opportunity to read the manual and comment on your work.

Activity 4

Imagine your family is having a guest coming to live with them for a month. The guest will become involved in family life and will need to be aware of how the family functions. They will have to be informed about the roles and responsibilities of each member of the family and how everyone works together.

Create a Family Instruction Manual for the guest. It could include some of the following information:
- an introduction to the members of the family
- the roles and responsibilities of each family member
- agreed rules of the house
- details of the family's daily routines
- details of how any disagreements or issues of concern are resolved.

We go through several stages during our life. This is known as the life cycle. There are five main stages in the life cycle.

Learning intentions

I am learning:

✓ what the stages in the LIFE CYCLE are
✓ examples of PHYSICAL, INTELLECTUAL, EMOTIONAL and SOCIAL NEEDS
✓ that needs change throughout our lives.

 Activity 1

Look at the picture above of the Robinson family. This family includes members at various stages in the life cycle. Can you identify what these different stages are? Write the stages down in order from the youngest to the oldest member. Also suggest an age range for each stage.

 Activity 2

Using your own family or a family from television, draw a picture to show members at various stages of the life cycle.

STAGES IN THE LIFE CYCLE

Baby/Toddler
(0–4years)

Older person
(65+ years)

Child
(4–11 years)

Adult
(18–65 years)

Adolescent
(11–18 years)

CHANGING NEEDS

As an individual gets older their needs change. Our needs are divided into four main categories:

Physical needs –	these are the basic requirements that we need to stay alive and healthy, such as food, water and warmth.
Intellectual needs –	these include the stimuli we need to keep our brain active, such as education, books and play.
Emotional needs –	these include our need for love, security and a sense of belonging; everything we need to make us feel happy and contented.
Social needs –	our need to be in contact with others, to form relationships and to be socially accepted can be met through friendships and hobbies, and through showing consideration to others.

Activity 3

a) Consider the list of needs in the word bank at the bottom of this page and decide what type of need each one is – physical, intellectual, emotional or social. Some needs could fit into more than one category.

b) When you have decided which category the needs fit into, copy the table below and complete it by inserting each need at the appropriate stage of the life cycle. For example, food is a physical need required at every stage of the life cycle. Starting school meets children's social needs as well as their intellectual needs.

	Baby/Toddler 0–4 years	Child 4–11 years	Adolescent 11–18 years	Adult 18–65 years	Older person 65+ years
Physical	Food	Food	Food	Food	Food
Intellectual		Starting school			
Social		Starting school			
Emotional					

Word Bank

Food	**Good manners**	*Security*
Toys	Nursery school	Examination
Education	education	preparation
Relationships	**Hygiene**	**Learning to read**
Sense of belonging	*Relaxation*	**and write**
Love	Social contact	Income
Warm home	**Healthcare**	Talking and listening
Books	**Hobbies**	*Career progression*
Safety	Confidence	**Discipline**
Play	*Starting school*	Routine
Bonding	Exercise	Independence
Clothing	**Self-worth**	**Contact with people**

REVIEW

 Complete the following:

a) Three things I learned through this chapter ...
b) Two things I enjoyed about this chapter ...
c) One thing I would still like to find out about ...

Learning intentions

I am learning:

- ✓ about the nutritional needs of a baby and toddler
- ✓ about the benefits of breastfeeding and how it meets a baby's nutritional needs
- ✓ the advantages and disadvantages of bottle feeding a baby
- ✓ about weaning and how to wean a baby successfully.

 ## Activity 1

a) Write down words that describe your immediate thoughts, feelings and opinions when you first look at a photograph like the one below of a mother breastfeeding her baby.

b) Why do you think this mother might have chosen to feed her baby in this way?

A baby needs food to survive. Breastfeeding is widely recognised as offering many benefits for babies and their mothers. The table below shows how aware a range of women are of the benefits associated with breastfeeding a baby.

 ## Activity 2

a) Which benefit were the women in this table most aware of?

b) Which benefit were mothers who did not breastfeed unaware of?

c) What percentage of breastfeeding mothers were aware that breastfeeding improves the intelligence of babies?

d) Were you aware of any of the benefits listed? If so, which ones had you heard of before?

This table shows how aware women are of some of the benefits associated with breastfeeding.

	All %	Breastfeeding mothers %	Non-breastfeeding mothers %	Women aged 15–44 with no children %
Reduces the risk of infection	42	62	44	43
Baby gets all required nutrients	63	77	54	63
Fewer prolonged colds in breastfed babies	16	11	30	16
Allergies less frequent in breastfed babies	8	12	4	10
Breastfed babies are more resistant to infections	20	40	17	28
Improved intelligence of breastfed babies	3	7	2	3
Death rates are lower among breastfed babies	3	5	-	5
Other	9	6	9	14

Source: 'Breastfeeding in Northern Ireland. A summary report on knowledge, attitudes and behaviour', published by the Health Promotion Agency for Northern Ireland, March 2003.

Activity 3

a) Select one of the benefits of breastfeeding from the table on page 42 and carry out research to find out more about it. Information is available on this topic from health centres, pharmacies, hospitals, libraries, mothers who have breastfed and on many internet sites, for example the Health Promotion Agency's www.breastfedbabies.org

b) Present your findings to the class.

Breastfeeding offers many other benefits for both mother and baby. A mother who breastfeeds will be at lower risk of ovarian and breast cancer, osteoporosis and type 2 diabetes. Feeding her baby will help to burn off excess weight after pregnancy – an extra 500 calories a day. Breastfeeding creates a close bond between mother and baby and is a very rewarding experience for both.

Other benefits include:
- breast milk is free
- it is easy for the baby to digest
- it is always at the correct temperature
- there is no need to prepare feeds and sterilise equipment
- the baby can be fed anywhere.

In Northern Ireland, many mothers have chosen not to breastfeed their babies for a number of reasons. However, this situation is changing and, as the graph on the right shows, the number of mothers who choose to breastfeed their babies is on the increase.

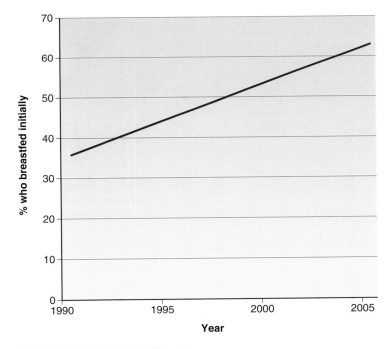

Incidence of breastfeeding in Northern Ireland, 1990–2005.

Activity 4

Discuss with your class why you think there are still mothers in Northern Ireland who do not breastfeed their babies.

Activity 5

Organise a class debate on the following statement: 'A mother should feel free to breastfeed her baby anywhere.'

Take into account the views expressed during the debate. Write down your personal feelings and opinions on this issue and draw your own conclusions.

BOTTLE FEEDING

A number of new mothers in Northern Ireland choose to bottle feed their baby with formula milk. Formula milk is made from cow's milk, with a lot of added vitamins and minerals. Babies who are bottle fed do not receive any of the health benefits of breastfeeding but can still develop a close bond if feeding is carefully done. There are advantages and disadvantages to bottle feeding a baby as shown in the diagram below.

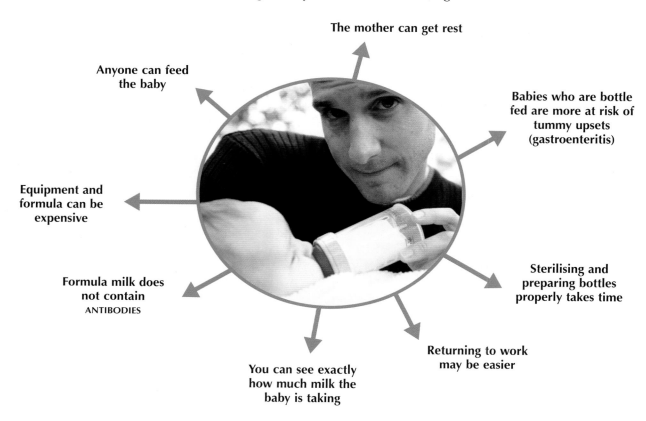

The mother can get rest

Anyone can feed the baby

Babies who are bottle fed are more at risk of tummy upsets (gastroenteritis)

Equipment and formula can be expensive

Formula milk does not contain ANTIBODIES

Sterilising and preparing bottles properly takes time

You can see exactly how much milk the baby is taking

Returning to work may be easier

Activity 6

The statements in the diagram above all relate to bottle feeding. Think about each statement and decide whether it is an advantage or disadvantage. You could record your answers as a table.

WEANING

Babies' nutritional needs change as they get older. Once a baby reaches six months, milk alone no longer supplies all the essential nutrients the baby needs in the required quantity. A baby may be drinking all their milk at each feed but this still does not provide enough calories to meet their growing needs. However, milk does remain an important part of a baby's diet.

WEANING is the gradual change from a diet consisting only of milk to a variety of solid foods. Health professionals recommend that babies are not introduced to solid foods before the age of six months, as early weaning can lead to health problems such as food allergies. The baby's digestive system is not mature enough to break down solid food before this age.

Ready, Steady, Wean!

Tips for successful weaning

- It is best to introduce one new food at a time.
- If the baby appears to dislike a food don't persist – wait a while and try again.
- Mince, purée, grate or mash foods appropriately to avoid choking.
- Be very aware of the amount of salt in food and never add salt.
- Never give a child nuts as these can cause allergies and are choking hazards.
- While weaning, babies should have breast or formula milk as their main drink.
- Introduce full fat cow's milk as their drink after the age of one year.
- Give the baby a variety of foods with different textures.
- Introduce raw fruit and vegetables to encourage the child to chew and to strengthen the teeth and gums.
- Never leave a baby unattended when eating in case of choking.

 Activity 7

Write an article for a parenting magazine on one aspect of feeding a baby or toddler.

You could select as your topic breastfeeding, bottle feeding or weaning. You will need to carry out research into your chosen topic and select the most appropriate information to include. Use a computer presentation package to present your article.

REVIEW

Complete the following sentences:

a) In this chapter I learned ...
b) I was surprised by ...
c) I was especially interested in ...
d) One thing I'm not sure about is ...
e) The main thing I would like to find out more about is ...
f) After this chapter I feel ...

Learning intentions

I am learning:

✓ about the nutritional needs of children
✓ how a healthy, balanced lunch can meet the nutritional needs of children
✓ how children can be encouraged to enjoy mealtimes
✓ to work with others in creating an effective advertising campaign to promote a new range of healthy breakfast cereals aimed at the children's market.

*safe*food is the Food Safety Promotion Board for Ireland. They promote food safety and carry out research. Occasionally, foods can become contaminated during the manufacturing process and have to be withdrawn from sale; the Board's role is to make sure consumers are informed.

 Activity 1

a) Discuss what message you think *safe*food is trying to get across by showing the lunch boxes below.
b) For many children the lunch box on the left would be a regular part of their daily diet. What problems could occur if this lunch is eaten regularly?

This poster is from a safefood campaign to encourage parents to reduce the amount of fatty and sugary foods in their children's diet. These foods include chocolate, biscuits and cakes. Currently these foods contribute a lot of fat to children's diets because children are eating on average twice the amount that would be considered healthy. The aim of the poster is to make people aware that there are health risks for children in later life if they eat too many foods high in fat. These health risks include an increased risk of heart disease, diabetes and cancer. This campaign was supported by practical advice on healthy eating at www.safefoodonline.com/lunchbox

THE ONE ON THE RIGHT IS ALMOST AS NUTRITIOUS.

Parents and carers who plan and pack a nutritious and healthy lunch give their children a balanced meal in the middle of the day.

Packing a healthy lunch for busy bodies

- Lunch boxes should be enjoyable.
- Children should be given a choice or encouraged to prepare their own lunch box.
- Lunch boxes should provide plenty of energy for busy children.
- The food should be easy for children to eat.
- Lunch boxes should contain a variety of foods from all the food groups.

A balanced lunchbox will consist of a range of foods from each of the five food groups in the correct proportions. Here are some ideas that could be used.

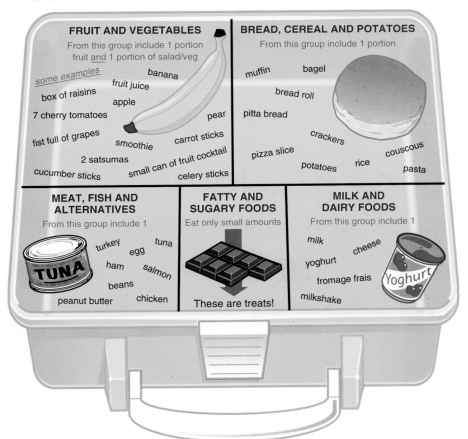

FRUIT AND VEGETABLES
From this group include 1 portion fruit and 1 portion of salad/veg
some examples
banana
fruit juice
box of raisins
apple
7 cherry tomatoes
pear
fist full of grapes
carrot sticks
smoothie
2 satsumas
small can of fruit cocktail
cucumber sticks
celery sticks

BREAD, CEREAL AND POTATOES
From this group include 1 portion
muffin
bagel
bread roll
pitta bread
crackers
pizza slice
couscous
potatoes
rice
pasta

MEAT, FISH AND ALTERNATIVES
From this group include 1
turkey
tuna
egg
ham
salmon
beans
peanut butter
chicken

FATTY AND SUGARY FOODS
Eat only small amounts
These are treats!

MILK AND DAIRY FOODS
From this group include 1
milk
cheese
yoghurt
fromage frais
milkshake

Activity 2

a) With a partner, discuss what you had for lunch when you were at primary school.

b) As a class work out what the most popular lunchtime foods were. How do these compare with the foods in the lunch box in the picture on page 46?

Activity 3

a) Using the tips for an ideal lunch box on the left, plan two possible lunches for a five-year-old child. For each lunch consider the advantages and disadvantages for the child. Use this analysis to decide which lunch to plan, prepare and serve.

b) Prepare and serve your packed lunch.

c) Compare your lunch with others in your class.
   - What are the strengths of your lunch?
   - How might you improve your lunch?

d) Describe how your lunch contributes to the nutritional needs of a child. Use the diagram on page 48 to help you.

NUTRITIONAL NEEDS OF A CHILD

Iron
Helps blood to stay healthy and helps to carry oxygen around the body.

Vitamin A
Helps to prevent night blindness in children.

Vitamin C
Reduces the risk of infections and helps iron absorption.

Calcium
Helps bones and teeth to develop and stay strong and healthy.

Vitamin D
Helps the body to absorb calcium and helps bones and teeth to be strong.

Carbohydrates
Provides energy for running around and rapid growth.

Fibre
Essential for a healthy digestive system.

Protein
Important for growth and repair of body cells.

MEALTIMES WITH CHILDREN

As well as preparing healthy lunch boxes, it is important to encourage children to eat healthily at home. Below are some suggestions how to do this.

Mealtimes = Happy Time

1 When possible eat together as a family with the television off to encourage conversation.

2 Parents and carers should lead by example and eat a balanced diet themselves.

3 Discourage snacking between meals and try to maintain regular meal times.

4 We all have likes and dislikes so don't force a child to eat something that they clearly dislike – perhaps try to disguise foods.

5 Don't let meal times become a battle ground – it may be a good idea to introduce a new food when the child is hungry and ready to eat.

6 Show children that cooking and meal times are fun by allowing them to help prepare and serve meals.

 **Activity 4**

As a class, discuss the tips given above for happy mealtimes. Suggest the reasons for the advice given and discuss the importance of these tips and how they can have a positive impact on young children at mealtimes.

ADVERTISING FOOD TO CHILDREN

Even though parents and carers may be making an effort to encourage healthy eating, their children are often exposed to irresponsible marketing of food.

As a result of the increase in childhood obesity and poor food choice by children and young people, there has been increasing concern over the way food that is high in fat, salt and sugar is advertised to children. As a result of these concerns action has been taken by Ofcom.

Ofcom is the independent regulator and competition authority for the UK communications industries, with responsibilities across television, radio, telecommunications and wireless communications services.

Restrictions put in place will mean that advertisements for food high in fat, salt and sugar should not be shown on television around programmes specifically made for children and teenagers. There are also proposals to prevent the use of celebrities and well-known television characters in advertisements targeted at primary school children. Promotional offers and nutritional health claims used in advertising to children will also be restricted.

  Activity 5

a) Get into groups and look at the advert on the top of page 51. Your task is to provide the sample that the advertising agency is asking for.

b) First decide what a successful advertising campaign would include. Discussing the following questions might help you.
- What makes a good advertisement?
- What makes an advertisement memorable?
- Does music or comedy help to sell a product?
- Do celebrities influence children?
- Does the product require attractive packaging?

c) As a result of your discussion design some sample advertising material to respond to the advert. Your material may include some of the following:
- packaging to attract young children, like those in the pictures on page 51
- a filmed advertisement to include a script and/or a jingle
- a script or recording of a radio advertisement
- a magazine or bill board advertisements
- money-off coupons.

d) Now create your advertising materials and present them to the rest of your class.

> **A lively child-friendly advertising agency seeks submissions from design companies who would like to be on its books.**
> Interested groups should provide a sample of their advertising materials promoting a new range of healthy breakfast cereals aimed at the children's market.

Some manufacturers aim their products at children.

REVIEW

a) As a group, decide which of the other groups' materials from Activity 5 were the most effective and will win the contract with the advertising agency.

b) Provide feedback to the class on the reasons for your choice of winner.

c) In your group review what you have learned from this activity and suggest some aspect that could be improved upon.

Learning intentions

I am learning:

- ✓ to understand some of the issues facing me as a teenager
- ✓ to select information that is appropriate to a variety of different tasks
- ✓ to review what I learn and think of ways to improve my work
- ✓ to be responsible for my own work when I work individually and with others.

A

Acne is a common worry for teenagers. Hormone changes stimulate oil glands in the skin, resulting in changes in the skin and hair condition. Good personal hygiene is vital during adolescence. Drinking plenty of water and eating plenty of fruit and vegetables are important for general health and in particular for healthy, clear skin.

B

Be active. Adolescence can be a very stressful time but getting involved in a range of activities can help you to cope with stress. This could be anything from taking a leisurely walk with friends to becoming involved in a sports club or team. As well as reducing stress levels, activity could help you make new friends, improve your self-esteem and become more healthy. Inactivity can lead to long-term health problems such as obesity and coronary heart disease so it is important to get active when you are young.

 Activity 1

a) Carry out research into the leisure facilities in your local area.
b) Use the results of your research to write up a newspaper article for your local newspaper on your findings and aim to encourage the reader to become more physically active.

C

'I **can** do it.' For many reasons a teenager's self-esteem may be low. High self-esteem and self-confidence are important to enable you to face the many challenges ahead. You need to feel confident enough to make many important decisions and sometimes accept mistakes and deal with failure. A positive attitude is something that will help in many situations. Remember – success begins with **can**, not can't.

D

Diet is the food that is eaten by an individual. Teenagers are going through a period of intense growth and development so it is essential that they follow a healthy, balanced diet. You should aim to follow the guidelines given in the Balance of Good Health to help you look good, feel great and enjoy life.

- Enjoy your food.
- Eat a variety of different foods.
- Eat the right amount to be a healthy weight.
- Eat plenty of foods rich in starch and fibre.
- Don't eat too much fat.
- Don't eat sugary foods too often.
- Look after the vitamins in your food.

Teenagers should use the five-portion plate illustrated below to help them choose a healthy balanced diet.

It is important to choose a balanced diet.

Activity 2

In groups create a collage of media images that you feel could influence a young person to become unhappy with their body image. When completed, move around the room to view the work of other groups in your class.

E

There are two main types of **eating disorder** – anorexia nervosa and bulimia nervosa. A person affected by either of these eating disorders becomes obsessed with weight loss. The image they have in their mind of themselves becomes distorted and they cannot see how thin they really are. Eating disorders are more common now than ever before.

There are many factors that may contribute towards a young person developing an eating disorder. The media and how they portray body image can be an influencing factor.

Activity 3

Find out more about one of the eating disorders and the effect it has on the life of the sufferer and their family. Carry out research using internet sites such as the Eating Disorders Association (www.edauk.com).

F

For teenagers, **friends** are very important. Good friends should offer support, loyalty and encouragement. Friends should be there through any situation and be honest and trustworthy. Friendship is all about giving and taking. For a teenager who finds it difficult to make friends, joining a club or group is a great way to meet new people.

 Activity 4

Write a 'WANTED' advert for a new friend. Include ideal qualities you would expect from a good friend. Are looks and image important to you or is personality and character more crucial?

G

Have a good **giggle**. Laughter has many benefits including reducing stress hormones, exercising facial muscles and bringing people together. When we laugh our body releases endorphins, which are a natural pain killer and make us feel better. Laughing together with other people makes us more sociable, less reserved and more outgoing. Growing up can be difficult enough at times, so make sure you have a good giggle as often as you can.

Teenagers having a good giggle.

H

Hobbies can be enjoyed on your own or with other people. They can allow you to develop new skills and meet new people. It is important to keep your mind active and to spend time doing an activity you really enjoy. Hobbies can help to meet your changing physical, emotional, intellectual and social needs and may even help you when you are looking for a job.

I

Increased **independence** is something that all teenagers want. Becoming more independent brings with it more responsibility. You might be allowed to make some decisions about the food that is available at home, and you could help to prepare meals for yourself or even for the whole family. You could be given responsibility for some household chores and be in control of your own living space. Many teenagers like to express themselves through choice of clothing and hairstyle and this gives them some independence. It may eventually be possible for you to have your own key for your home and to have a part-time job, which will help you to learn how to manage your own money.

J

Many teenagers have part-time and holiday **jobs**. Once you are sixteen years old you are entitled to be paid the National Minimum Wage. Information on this is available from HM Revenue and Customs and the Citizens Advice Bureau.

K

Kilojoules is how energy is measured. If we consume too much energy from food and drink and don't use it, the excess is stored as fat and this could make us overweight. Teenagers should aim to maintain a healthy weight for their height as this will contribute to overall good health.

Love is in the air!

L

Love is in the air! There are different types of love including parental love, brotherly/sisterly love, romantic love and love between friends. The first experience of romantic love often happens during adolescence and this can be an emotional rollercoaster. Teenagers need a lot of support from friends and family at this time and it is important that they are able to confide in someone and express their feelings and emotions.

M

Money can come from pocket money, presents or from a part-time job. A personal budget will allow you to plan how to spend your income and prioritise your needs and wants. Teenagers need to take on the responsibility of balancing their income and spending and should develop the habit of saving some money.

 Activity 5

Individually create a poem or a rap on the theme of LOVE. Be prepared to perform this to your class!

N

The requirements for some **nutrients** increase during adolescence. As a teenager you are going through a period of rapid growth and development. The table below outlines some of the main nutrients that are essential to you at this stage in your life and some of the foods where you can find them.

What do I need?	Why do I need it?	Where can I get it from?
Protein	For growth, repair and maintenance of the body	Meat Fish Dairy foods Eggs Pulses Cereals Nuts
Carbohydrates	For energy	Bread Pasta Rice Potatoes
Fat	For warmth For protection of vital organs For energy	Butter Dairy foods Eggs Meat Cakes Biscuits
Calcium	For strong bones and teeth To reduce the risk of osteoporosis later in life	Milk Yoghurt Cheese
Iron	For healthy blood Particularly important for girls to prevent anaemia	Red meat Green leafy vegetables Dried fruit Pulses Fortified cereals
Vitamin C	Helps to absorb iron Important for healing wounds	Oranges Lemons Blackcurrants Kiwi Broccoli Green peppers
Vitamin D	Works with calcium to form strong bones and teeth	Sunshine Oily fish Margarine Eggs Liver Cheese

O

Osteoporosis is also known as 'brittle bone disease'. It is caused by a gradual loss of calcium from bones and mainly affects older people. However, teenagers can reduce the risk of developing this condition later in their lives by eating plenty of foods rich in calcium and Vitamin D. Exercise such as walking and running will help to keep bones strong.

P

The relationship that you have with your **parents** or carers may change, as your friends and what they think can become more important. However, it is very important to maintain your relationship with your parents/carers. They will usually be able to support you emotionally as well as physically as you mature and become an adult. Being able to talk openly and honestly with your parents/carers is often a difficult part of growing up. It is important to spend some time together regularly, maybe over a meal, so that each of you knows what the other is going through and can be of mutual support.

Q

Qualifications can contribute to your overall success in later life and there are many opportunities to gain qualifications during your teenage years (although it is possible to add to your qualifications throughout life). Motivation and self-discipline will help to ensure your success and gaining qualifications of any type will enhance your self-esteem and help you to feel good about yourself.

R

Relaxation is an important part of a healthy, balanced lifestyle. There are many ways to relax, including playing sport, taking a walk with friends, watching television, reading a book or playing computer games.

Gaining qualifications can open up many opportunities.

S

For most teenagers an active **social life** is important. Socialising with friends is a good way to relax, but you need to balance this time with time spent in the company of your family and completing school work. Think carefully about how and where you spend your time with your friends. Be aware of negative peer pressure that could influence you into becoming involved in risky or dangerous behaviour.

T

It's good to **talk**. There are many issues to face as you move through adolescence and it is very important that you don't bottle up your feelings. This is not healthy. There are many organisations available to support teenagers if you ever feel you cannot talk to friends, family or someone at school.

Preparing a vegetarian meal.

Activity 6

a) In pairs plan, prepare, cook and serve a snack suitable for a teenager who is a lacto–vegetarian. You need to show reasons for your choice and explain how your chosen snack will meet the nutritional needs of a teenager.

b) Ask your partner to evaluate your performance during this activity and suggest one way to improve your work.

U

You are **unique**. There is no one else in the world like you, there never has been and there never will be! Some people are very talented in many areas while others aren't particularly brilliant at any one thing. However, we all have an important part to play and a contribution to make to the lives of others. It is important that you make the most of who you are and understand that you are an important, unique individual.

V

There are two main types of **vegetarian** diet:
- Lacto-vegetarians do not eat meat, poultry or fish; however, they will eat animal products such as cheese, yoghurt and milk.
- Vegans do not eat any form of meat, including fish and poultry, or any products that come from animals.

Many teenagers choose to follow a vegetarian diet. They may do so for all or some of the following reasons:
- They believe that the production of meat involves cruelty to animals.
- They dislike the taste of meat.
- They believe a vegetarian diet will improve their health.
- Their religious beliefs prevent them from eating meat.
- They believe techniques used in producing meat are damaging to the environment.
- They are influenced by their family or by other people around them.

Vegetarian diets can be a very healthy option if planned carefully. As adolescence is a period of rapid growth and development, a teenage vegetarian should take extra care to ensure that they have a balanced diet containing all the essential nutrients in the required amounts.

Complete **well-being** is important and involves physical, emotional, social, intellectual and spiritual development. As a teenager it is important that you consider all these areas of your life to enable you to enjoy total well-being.

Your teens are a very precious and **eXciting** time of life. Be positive and make the most of it.

Just be **yourself**! Sometimes it is difficult for teenagers to be themselves. You may be influenced by your peers or by the media, but it is important to have a clear idea of your responsibilities and how you should behave towards yourself and others. Don't be afraid to be honest and true to yourself ... people will respect you for it.

Z

ZZZZZZZ – during adolescence it is very important that you get enough sleep. The experts recommend eight hours every night.

  Activity 7

a) In groups, select a variety of issues that you are interested in from this chapter, such as eating disorders, vegetarianism, hobbies, personal budgeting or relationships. Individually write a letter on one issue that could appear on a problem page in a teenage magazine. Within your group write an appropriate response to each letter.

b) The editor of the magazine wants to include an up-to-date list of organisations that could support teenagers in a variety of situations. Carry out research to find out about local organisations that could support teenagers for the issue you chose in part a) of this activity. Provide a list of organisations, how they can be contacted and a brief description of what they do.

REVIEW

Complete the following:
a) Three things I learned through this chapter ...
b) Two things I enjoyed about this chapter ...
c) One thing I would still like to find out about ...

Learning intentions

I am learning:

✓ about the nutritional needs of a pregnant woman
✓ about the foods that a pregnant woman should avoid eating
✓ to work with a partner to plan meals for a pregnant woman.

During adulthood, nutritional needs change because the body is no longer growing. Nutrients such as protein and calcium are no longer needed for growth but for the repair and maintenance of body cells. Adults have different energy and nutritional needs depending on their gender, body size and level of physical activity.

During pregnancy and breastfeeding a woman's needs also change to take account of the developing baby. The diet needs to be high in nutrients during pregnancy as the baby depends on the mother's body to provide everything it needs to grow and develop.

NUTRITIONAL NEEDS OF A PREGNANT WOMAN

Plenty of carbohydrate foods for energy.

Wholemeal/wholegrain varieties of pasta, breakfast cereals and bread to provide dietary fibre and help prevent constipation, which can be a problem in pregnancy.

A little extra protein to allow for the growth of the developing baby, as well as the repair and replacement of cells for the mother.

FOLIC ACID is vital for the healthy development of the baby.

Calcium is needed to keep the mother's bones healthy and is important for the formation of the baby's bones and teeth.

Extra iron is needed for the mother to prevent anaemia and for the baby to store for use in the first few months of its life.

A good supply of vitamins is needed, particularly vitamin C for iron absorption and Vitamin D to help absorb calcium for teeth and bone formation.

 Activity 1

Nicky in the diagram on the right is expecting her first child. Look at her nutritional needs and make a list of foods that she could eat to help her have a healthy pregnancy and a healthy baby.

Eating for a healthy baby

Pregnancy is such an exciting time and it is important that you look after yourself. Your body has to work hard and in this article we give you tips on how to take care of yourself, with advice on eating well.

- A balanced diet is important in order to receive all the nutrients that are needed for both you and your baby. Your body will take what it needs, so make sure you have enough of the essential nutrients for both of you – if you don't, it's your health that will suffer.

- You do not need to 'eat for two'. Eating too much can lead to you putting on extra weight, which can be difficult to lose after the baby is born.

- Folic acid is vital. Research has shown that the vitamin folate taken before pregnancy and up until the twelfth week can reduce the risk of spina bifida and other neural tube defects. For this reason you should take extra folate. This should be taken in the form of 400 mg supplements, called folic acid, which are available from pharmacies, the supermarket or on prescription from your doctor. Folate can also be found in green, leafy vegetables such as spinach and broccoli, in fortified breakfast cereals and in bread.

- You need to be careful with other vitamin supplements during pregnancy as large doses of some vitamins can harm you or your baby. Too much vitamin A from animal sources such as liver can increase the risk of birth defects.

- During pregnancy it is important to avoid eating pâté, soft ripened cheeses such as brie, blue-veined cheeses, unpasteurised milk and products made from it. It is also vital that cook-chilled products are piping hot. These foods may contain bacteria called listeria that can cause miscarriage or premature birth.

- Foods containing raw egg such as mayonnaise and home-made ice-cream, and undercooked chicken should be avoided. These foods can cause salmonella food poisoning, which can be particularly harmful for a pregnant woman and her baby.

- TOXOPLASMOSIS is a tiny parasite that can cause blindness or brain damage in a baby. Care should be taken with unpasteurised milk and products made from it, and with raw or undercooked meats. It is also important to wash all fruit and vegetables before eating and to wash your hands after handling raw meat.

- If you or someone in your family has a peanut allergy, eating peanuts during pregnancy may increase the chances of your baby developing a potentially dangerous allergy to peanuts. It is therefore advisable to avoid eating nuts throughout pregnancy.

- Coffee, tea and cola all contain caffeine, which is a stimulant. Large quantities may cause problems for babies. Drink decaffeinated drinks or fruit teas as an alternative.

 **Activity 2**

Test your knowledge!
After reading pages 60–61 try this quick quiz to find out what you know about eating for a healthy pregnancy.

1. A pregnant women needs a good supply of calcium for:
   a) healthy blood
   b) making her bones grow
   c) helping the unborn baby's bones to develop?

2. Which of the following is a good source of iron for a pregnant woman:
   a) liver
   b) red meat
   c) strawberries?

3. Which of the following foods should a pregnant woman avoid eating:
   a) wholemeal bread
   b) unpasteurised milk
   c) cake?

4. Which of the following foods can cause listeria:
   a) pâté
   b) Cheddar cheese
   c) bread?

5. Folic acid should be taken up until:
   a) sixth week of pregnancy
   b) twelfth week of pregnancy
   c) third week of pregnancy?

6. Pregnant women should be careful taking vitamin supplements because:
   a) they are very expensive
   b) they don't contain all the vitamins she needs
   c) they can be dangerous in high doses?

7. Which of the following contains caffeine:
   a) coffee, tea and cola
   b) apple juice, water and herbal tea

   c) milk, orange juice and pineapple juice?

8. Toxoplasmosis can cause:
   a) headaches for the mother
   b) constipation
   c) blindness or brain damage in the baby?

9. Which of the following foods are good sources of folic acid:
   a) fortified breakfast cereals and broccoli
   b) cheese and yoghurt
   c) apples and grapes?

10. A little extra protein is needed during pregnancy:
    a) to help the mother grow
    b) to protect the mother's eyesight
    c) for the growth of the baby?

Case study

Laura and Martin have just found out that they are expecting their first child. Laura is a vegetarian. Laura's grandmother has been giving Laura a lot of advice about what she should and shouldn't be eating. She is telling Laura that she should be eating for two and should start eating some meat. Laura has been reading books and magazines on pregnancy and is very confused about the advice being given. Laura needs your help.

  Activity 3

a) Read the case study and using ICT, create a leaflet that advises Laura about foods to eat and foods to avoid throughout her pregnancy to help ensure her baby gets the best start to life.

b) In pairs, plan a day's menu for Laura. Take account of her dietary needs. Plan, prepare, cook and serve a meal for Laura.

REVIEW

 a) Choose a partner and decide on a set of criteria for what makes a good leaflet.

b) Take turns at reading each other's leaflets from Activity 3. Using your criteria, tell each other about the strengths of the leaflet and any ways in which you feel they could improve.

15 PARENT POWER

Becoming a parent is something most people feel they are not prepared for. Having children is a major life-changing event and brings with it many new responsibilities. Becoming a parent is one of the most exhausting, emotional, difficult, yet wonderful experiences anyone could have.

Learning intentions

I am learning:

✓ how being a parent can change your life
✓ to be aware of the skills necessary to become a good parent
✓ how parents can cope in a range of situations
✓ to work effectively with others to plan and develop a parenting course

Case study

Jessica and David have just had a baby boy called Callum. He is their first child. They both work full-time and Jessica is planning to return to work after her maternity leave. At times she finds it quite difficult being a new mum, although David helps out as much as he can. Her parents live quite close by and she has other friends who also have young children.

Activity 1

a) Discuss with your class other thoughts and feelings that Jessica and David may have.
b) How has having Callum changed their lives?

Jo Frost, Supernanny.

EFFECTIVE PARENTING

There is no such thing as a perfect parent but everyone can be a good parent. There are many skills involved in becoming a good parent and these can be learned and practised. Jo Frost, known as Supernanny, is an experienced nanny with over fifteen years of experience with unruly and badly behaved children. She has featured in her own television programmes in the UK and USA and has published books for parents wanting to become effective parents.

The following is a list of her Top Ten Rules on how to be an effective parent.

MY TOP TEN RULES

1. PRAISE AND REWARDS
The best rewards are attention, praise and love. Sweets, treats and toys are not necessary as rewards. A star chart or a special outing can back up a pattern of good behaviour.

2. CONSISTENCY
Once you have made a rule, don't change it for the sake of a quiet life or because you're embarrassed. Make sure that everyone – which includes carers and your partner – keeps to the same rules as well. A rule is a rule is a rule.

3. ROUTINE
Keep your home in basic order and maintain a routine. Set times for waking, meals, bath and bed are the cornerstones of family life. Once a routine is in place, you can be a little flexible, if you're on holiday, for example. It's a framework, but it doesn't have to be rigid.

4. BOUNDARIES
Children need to know there are limits to their behaviour – which means what is acceptable and what is not. You need to set rules and tell them what you expect.

5. DISCIPLINE
You can only keep the boundaries in place by discipline. This means firm and fair control. It may just take an authoritative voice and a warning to get the message across. Otherwise, there are other techniques you can use, none of which involve punishment.

6. WARNINGS
There are two kinds of warning. One tells a child what's coming next – you're the Speaking Clock telling her that bathtime is coming up soon, or that you're getting near to putting her lunch on the table. The other is a warning for bad behaviour. That gives her the chance to correct her behaviour without any further discipline.

7. EXPLANATIONS
A small child can't understand how you want him to behave unless you tell him. Show and tell to get the message across. Don't reason or make it too complicated – just state the obvious. When you are disciplining a child, explain in a way that is appropriate for his age. Ask him if he understands the reason why he has been disciplined so that the message hits home.

8. RESTRAINT
Keep cool. You're the parent and you're in charge. Don't answer a tantrum by a display of anger or respond to shouting by shouting back. You're the adult here. Don't let them wind you up.

9. RESPONSIBILITY
Childhood is all about growing up. Let them. Allow them to do small, achievable things to boost their self-confidence and learn the necessary life and social skills. Get them involved in family life. But make sure your expectations are reasonable. Don't set them up for failure.

10. RELAXATION
Quality time is important for everyone, including yourself. Let your child unwind at bedtime with a story and cuddles. Make sure you, your partner and your other kids have quality time for individual attention.

 **Activity 2**

a) In groups read and consider the following descriptions of common situations that can happen in families with young children. Use the rules given by Supernanny on page 64 to help you to decide how you would deal with each situation.

b) Share your opinions within your group and if possible reach an agreement on the best way to handle each situation. Share your ideas with the rest of your class.

Situations

1. Four-year-old Niamh, her baby brother Neill and their mum visit the supermarket every week. Niamh gets bored and begins to run around. Niamh's mum threatens, 'If you don't stop running around, you will not get sweets at the end'. Niamh continues to run around and when they get to the checkout, their mum buys both Niamh and Neill some sweets. Without saying a word she hands them over. Niamh is not surprised – this always happens.

2. Aidan is five and has a big sister called Ellen. Ellen makes her own packed lunch every morning and Aidan has decided he wants to do the same. He makes a real mess of the kitchen and ends up with lumps of torn bread and cheese. Aidan doesn't seem to mind but his mum ends up getting cross and makes another sandwich for him. Ellen is fed up as she is late for school and Aidan starts to cry.

3. Ben's dad Mark has promised to take him to a football match on Saturday. At the last minute Mark is asked to work overtime, so to earn extra money for the family, Mark agrees to do the shift. Ben is confused the next morning to find that his dad has gone to work. His mum explains the situation to Ben but he is really upset.

REVIEW

 a) Complete the following;
  • Three things I learned through this chapter are ...
• Two things I enjoyed about this chapter are ...
• One thing I would still like to find out about is ...
b) Draw up a list of keywords relevant to the topic of parenting.

  Activity 3

It could be easy to believe that parenting will come naturally. Most parents learn as they go along with help from friends and family. They can still benefit, though, from learning parenting skills in a more structured way.

Jessica and David have decided to enrol in a parenting class that is being run in a local church hall.

Your group has been asked to plan and develop a parenting course for this class.

a) Decide on the most useful and relevant topics for new parents. You could include some ideas from Supernanny's Top Ten Rules, as well as topics such as feeding, bathing and nursery equipment.

b) Ensure that each group member takes personal responsibility for carrying out research and developing a topic.

c) Produce an information pack that will be used to deliver the parenting course.

d) To inform new parents about the course and advertise it, design a flyer to be distributed to homes in the local area.

Learning intentions

I am learning:

- ✓ about some of the issues facing older people
- ✓ about the nutritional needs of older people
- ✓ to work with a partner to plan, prepare, cook and serve a meal suitable for an older person.

A

B

C

D

 Activity 1

a) Study the photographs above and write an appropriate caption for each.

b) Compare and contrast your captions with others in your class.

The older, 65-plus age group is the largest and fastest-growing sector of our society. People aged 65 and over are no longer considered 'old', and many, such as some of those in the photographs opposite, still enjoy a happy, active and busy life.

The main factors for living longer are eating well and staying active. Staying active keeps the brain alert, keeps muscles fit and can lead to a more positive mental attitude, which improves self-confidence and the ability to cope with stressful events. Having the correct diet is more important than ever once you are over 65, as it reduces the risk of cancer and heart disease.

NUTRITIONAL NEEDS OF OLDER PEOPLE (65-PLUS)

Fat intake needs to be reduced to avoid becoming overweight.

Reduce carbohydrate intake as energy requirements are lower.

Increase the intake of fibre to prevent constipation.

Protein is needed for repair of body cells.

Iron is needed to reduce the risk of anaemia.

Vitamin C is needed to help prevent infections, for the proper healing of wounds and to assist in absorption of iron.

Calcium is needed to maintain bone strength.

Vitamin D is needed to help the body absorb calcium.

Eat to beat old age!

- Older people may be less active than younger people, so calorie intake should be cut back as energy requirements are lower.
- To help avoid too much weight gain, it's important to reduce saturated fat intake and keep active.
- Older people may have little appetite, for various reasons. It is important to eat highly nutritious small meals or snacks regularly.
- Many older people manage on low incomes, so the range of food they can afford is limited. It is important to shop wisely.
- Living alone, suffering bereavement or being housebound can result in a lack of interest in food. Eating in company could increase enjoyment of food. Many lunch clubs or day centres provide meals and the company of others.

- Some older people may not have the necessary skills or physical capability to prepare and cook meals. This is another reason for joining a lunch club or day centre.
- Some people may find food becomes less appetising as they get older. Using a variety of herbs and seasoning will improve the flavour of food.
- Older people who are housebound and have no exposure to sunlight may be at risk of a vitamin D deficiency. Doctors may advise them to take a vitamin D supplement.
- It is important to eat five portions of fruit and vegetables every day. They are full of vitamins, minerals and dietary fibre.
- Food should continue to be an important and enjoyable aspect of life.

Elderly people enjoying lunch together at a day centre.

Activity 2

Using the information on pages 67 and 68, write a script for a local radio programme featuring useful hints and tips for older people when shopping, storing, preparing and cooking food.

DIFFICULTIES FACED BY OLDER PEOPLE

Hugh is one of the older people in Northern Ireland whose income is reduced. Hugh relies on the state pension as his only source of income.

Case study

Name: Hugh Rea
Lives: Co. Down
Age: 82 years old
Marital status: widower

Hugh is a farmer who was married to Iris for 54 years. Sadly, Iris recently died. Hugh now lives alone in the farmhouse in a rural area in Co. Down.

Hugh and his wife had very traditional roles and he is finding it very difficult to adjust to his new situation.

  **Activity 3**

a) With a partner, create a bank of words that could be used to describe how Hugh is feeling.
b) Identify some of the difficulties Hugh may be having in adapting to his new situation.
c) In pairs, plan a day's menu for Hugh. Take account of his nutritional needs. Plan, prepare, cook and serve a meal for Hugh.

REVIEW

a) Identify the skills you used when planning, preparing, cooking and serving a meal for Hugh in Activity 3.
b) Suggest ways you could improve upon your practical cooking skills.

Learning intentions

Learning intentions

I am learning:

✓ to explore strategies for coping with family situations
✓ to work with others to create resources to suit different people in a variety of situations

 ## Activity 1

Read the problem page letters below. Before you read Real Life's responses, work in pairs to decide what you think a good response to the problem would be. Then read the response and answer the following questions:

a) Do you think that Real Life's advice will work? Give reasons for your answers.
b) Did you come up with a different response from Real Life? If so, which advice do you think is better – yours or Real Life's? Give reasons.
c) How useful do you think problem pages in magazines are?

Dear Real Life ...

Got a concern about something that is happening in your family? That's real life. All families face challenges and it is important to learn how to cope. Write to Real Life, share your experiences and get some good advice.

She gets right on my nerves

My younger sister Julie is 12 and she is really getting on my nerves. It's got to the stage now where we can't look at each other without physically fighting. We have to share a bedroom, which causes lots of problems. She is so untidy and leaves her stuff all over the place and I can't bring my friends into my room as she is always there. I have just started a part-time job and have bought some new CDs and clothes. She uses them as if they are hers and never asks. I am getting really fed up and mum doesn't see what the problem is. She always takes her side as she is the youngest. Living in our family has become really miserable for me. I feel that everyone is against me and can't see my side. What can I do?
Natasha, 14.

Real Life says ...

What you are experiencing is known as sibling rivalry and is a very common difficulty within families. Brothers and sisters argue over having their own space, getting attention or out of jealousy. There's nothing wrong with a bit of healthy competition, but obviously this is really getting you down. Here are a few coping strategies that you can use to help you deal with this situation.

■ You can tackle this situation by letting your sister know how you feel – talk to her when you are both calm. Communication is vital. You might even find that it gets her down too and that a stronger relationship between you may develop.

■ Make it clear to your sister what actually bothers you and try to reach a compromise. Are there some items of clothing that both of you could share? Could you draw up a rota to keep the bedroom tidy? Are there issues that aren't worth fighting over?

■ If you find yourself getting aggressive over the slightest thing, it's time to take a deep breath to control your anger – fighting won't help, it just creates more hurt and anger.

■ You need to talk to your mum about how you feel, as all this arguing may also be upsetting her.

Being best buddies with your sister isn't compulsory, but MUTUAL RESPECT should be. Have a go and hopefully your situation will improve.

They're too strict!

My mum and dad are far too protective. They won't allow me to go into town with my mates at the weekend. I am only allowed out one night during the week and even then I am always the first one who has to go home. I get on really well with my mum and dad and respect them completely but it is really embarrassing when they insist on collecting me wherever I go. How can I make them understand that I need a bit more freedom?
Gareth, 14.

Real Life says ...

It's often difficult for parents to learn to let go and allow their teenager a little more independence. It's good to hear that you have a good relationship with your parents and it should be easy to talk to your mum and dad to find out why they have a problem with you doing these things. I suspect that they feel that schoolwork and your ability to concentrate at school is important and this is why they have rules about you staying in during the week. They may be concerned about your safety when you are in town and prefer to make sure you get home safe. Gareth, you may not always feel it but you are fortunate to have parents who care about you in this way – so build on this. To cope with this issue you should talk to your mum and dad explaining your concern. Try to compromise and meet them halfway and hopefully they will soon realise that you are growing up and need more independence.

My parents are splitting up

My parents are getting divorced and I need some advice on how to deal with it. Some of my friends have been in the same situation and have seemed to cope fine but I am finding it really hard and seem to cry all the time. I am worried and scared about what is going to happen and I feel as if

I'm stuck in the middle. I love both my mum and dad and wonder who I am going to live with when this is all over – I don't want to take sides. I can't help feeling that some of this must be my fault, but I can't really think what I've done. Please help me.
Orla, 12.

Real Life says ...

Orla, you're not alone. Divorce affects everybody differently, so don't be surprised that your feelings are mixed up. You may feel shocked, angry, upset, confused, guilty, worried, relieved, scared and as you say, sometimes even like it's your fault. The fact that your parents' feelings towards each other have changed has nothing to do with you – it doesn't mean they've changed the way they feel about you. Discuss with your parents how you are feeling and what your future living arrangements will be. It is possible to have both parents involved in your life. There are people you can talk to who may help you cope with this family situation. Talk to your friends and get it off your chest, as some of them have been through it too, and can share their experiences with you. You could talk to other people in your family, a trusted teacher or another adult you know well and can trust. Childline can offer advice and they can put you in touch with other helpful organisations in your area. We hope it all works out for the best.

Activity 2

Tanya is like many young teenagers in Northern Ireland who care for a parent or relative.

a) In pairs, identify some coping strategies that would help Tanya and her family in this situation. Carry out research to find out about some organisations that could offer support and advice for young carers such as Tanya.

b) Write 'Real Life's' reply to Tanya's situation.

 **Activity 3**

Your school is developing a student support service that will offer advice to pupils on many issues, including coping strategies to use within a range of family situations.

a) As a class consider family situations that can be challenging.

b) In groups select one of these and create resources that would help teenagers in your school who may be facing challenging situations in the home.

You could include:
- leaflets for a stand
- information for the student support service website
- fact sheets for distribution
- articles for your school magazine or work sheets for use in the classroom.

c) Display the resources you have produced in your classroom.

REVIEW

Complete the following sentences:

a) In this chapter I learned …
b) I was surprised by …
c) I was especially interested in …
d) One thing I'm not sure about is …
e) The main thing I would like to find out more about is …
f) After this chapter I feel …

Learning intentions

I am learning:

✓ about the main expenses of having a home
✓ how to create a monthly household BUDGET
✓ about the factors that may influence us when shopping for food
✓ to work with others to compare ready-made meals with a homemade version.

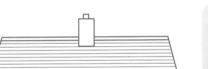

A mortgage is an amount of money borrowed from a bank or building society used to buy a house. This is repaid over a long period of time, usually 25 years. Payments are made monthly.

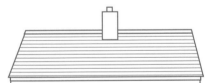

Rent is paid to a landlord who owns the property. This can be paid weekly or monthly.

 Activity 1

Paul has just moved into his first home by himself. With a partner, think of five questions you would like to ask him about his move.

At some stage most people set up their own home. This is a big financial commitment, which should be carefully planned. Paying for a home means either having a MORTGAGE or paying RENT to a landlord.

Paul has decided to rent a house. Paying your mortgage or rent is one of the main household costs but not the only one.

 Activity 2

a) With a partner examine the picture opposite. Make a list of all the household expenses you see.
b) Now share your answers with the rest of the class and make an overall class list.
c) As a class try to list the monthly expenses in order from most expensive to least expensive. You could use the information on page 76 to help you. Check your list by asking an adult.

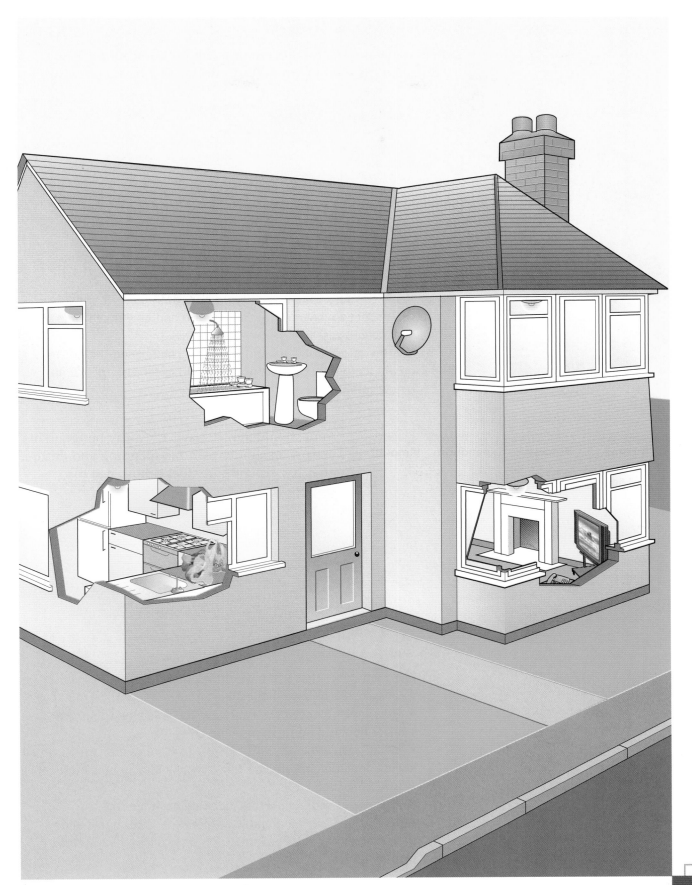

SETTING A BUDGET

Before making the final decision to set up home alone, Paul contacted his friend who moved into his first home last year.

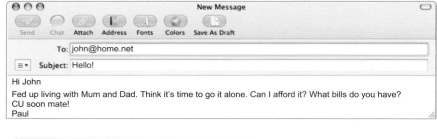

To: john@home.net

Subject: Hello!

Hi John
Fed up living with Mum and Dad. Think it's time to go it alone. Can I afford it? What bills do you have? CU soon mate!
Paul

Telephone bill Please pay **£33.00**

TELEVISION LICENCE Please pay **£11.00**

Gas Please pay **£50.00**

Electricity bill Please pay **£20.00**

Digital TV Please pay **£20.00**

Rent **£300.00**

CUT PRICE SUPERMARKET **£300.00**

Activity 3

a) Reply to Paul's e-mail giving him information on what bills he can expect to have to pay each month and how much each of them could cost him.
b) Use the information you gathered and the bills on the left to create a monthly budget for Paul using Excel. Use the format below to help you.

Paul should aim to have a healthy budget. This means he should plan his spending and ensure that his expenditure does not exceed his INCOME.

	A	B	C	D
1	**Income**	**Amount**	**Expenditure**	**Amount**
2				
3	Full-time job	£950	Gas	£50
4				
5				
6				
7				
8	Total			
9	Balance			

Activity 4

a) Use the budget that you have drawn up for Paul in Activity 3 to answer the following questions:
   • How much money does Paul have left to spend each month after he has paid the household bills?
   • What other expenses is Paul likely to have each month?
   • How much money do you think he should allow for these other expenses?
   • How could Paul reduce his spending each month?
   • What should he be doing with money he does not spend?
b) In pairs design an advice leaflet for Paul to help him keep a healthy budget.

SHOPPING FOR ONE

One of the ways Paul could reduce his monthly expenditure is to spend less money on food.

Activity 5

What other factors does Paul need to keep in mind when shopping for his food? Complete the spider diagram.

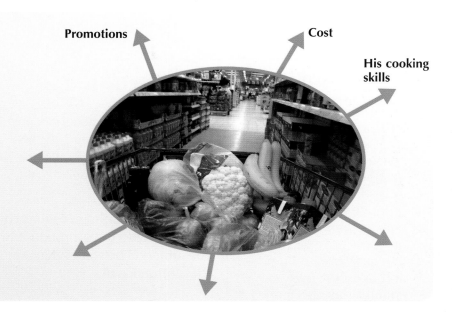

Promotions

Cost

His cooking skills

Activity 6

Paul can't decide if he should buy ready-made meals or make meals himself.

a) In groups plan, prepare, cook and serve a meal that you could compare with a ready-made version, for example lasagne, curry, pie.

b) Compare the meals by recording comments on the features listed in the table below.

Features	Comment on ready-made meal	Comment on your group's meal
Cost		
Size		
Taste		
Smell		
Texture		
Ease of preparation		
Cooking and preparation time		

c) Use your results to present arguments for and against using ready-made meals.

d) Come to a conclusion – do you think Paul should buy these ready-made meals or make the meal himself? Give reasons for your answer.

REVIEW

 Complete the following sentences.

a) In this chapter I learned …

b) I was surprised by …

c) I was especially interested in …

d) One thing I'm not sure about is …

e) The main thing I would like to find out more about is …

f) After this chapter I feel …

Learning intentions

I am learning:

- ✓ what a consumer is
- ✓ what influences a consumer when shopping
- ✓ to work with others to produce an awareness-raising campaign about one ETHICAL issue
- ✓ to examine evidence and draw my own conclusions about an ethical issue influencing consumers.

 Activity 1

Tell your partner about one item you have recently bought. Why did you buy this item? Together think about why each of you made the choices you did and what made you choose this way. What influenced you?

Many factors influence what consumers buy. A consumer is someone who buys a product or uses a SERVICE. We are all consumers. The spider diagram shows some of the factors that influence us.

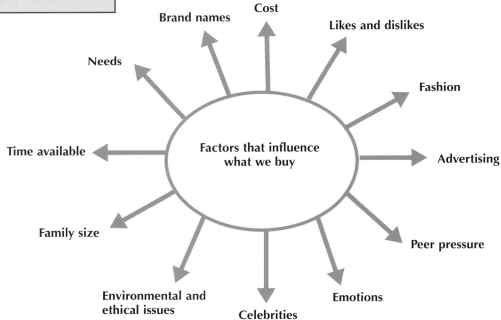

In this chapter you will focus on information that will enable you to make choices and decisions about what you buy in a more responsible way. The issues you will look at include FOOD MILES, recycling, FAIRTRADE, ORGANIC food and ANIMAL TESTING.

THE ETHICAL CONSUMER

As a teenage consumer you have many important decisions to make about what to buy and how to spend your money.

Is organic food better?

What should I buy?

Can this packet be recycled?

Has my shampoo been tested on animals?

Where in the world has my food come from?

Should I be concerned about farmers getting a fair price for their produce?

The questions the teenager is asking are questions that many consumers now consider before spending their money. Consumers are becoming more aware of ethical issues surrounding choices and decisions that they make. It is possible to take more responsibility over the choices you make and becoming a more ethical consumer can be simple.

Food Miles

Food miles are the measure of the distance a food travels from field to plate.

Some fish caught in Northern Ireland is sent to China for processing then back to the UK to be sold in supermarkets.

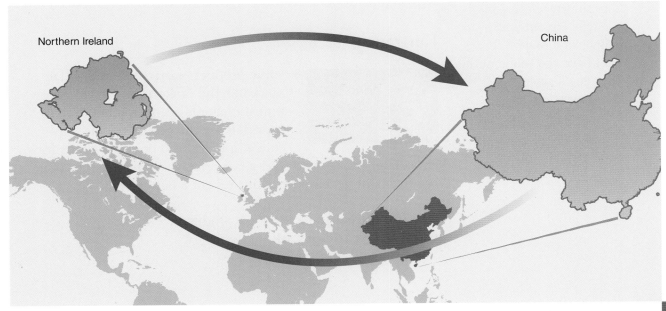

Northern Ireland

China

Activity 2

a) In pairs create a fact sheet on foods that are in season in the UK during one month of the year. Use www.bbc.co.uk/food to help with your research.

b) Display all the fact sheets for the different months of the year in your classroom or combine the fact sheets to create a booklet of information on foods that are in season throughout the year in the UK.

 Activity 3

a) Carry out research and identify up to ten organic products that are available in the supermarket.

b) Compare the cost of the organic products with other similar non-organic products. Present your findings in a table.

c) What have you found out?

d) Write down some advantages and disadvantages of buying organic foods.

It is quite possible that some of the food produced in Northern Ireland will travel to other parts of the world to be processed and then be sent back to Northern Ireland before it is sold. This happens with some fish caught in Northern Ireland. It is sent to China, where labour costs are much lower, for processing and is then returned to the United Kingdom to be sold in supermarkets.

Not only does this mean that local people are missing out on employment opportunities, it also has a huge impact on the environment due to the transport involved.

As an ethical consumer you should choose to buy more locally produced products and products that are in season.

Organic Food

Organic food is produced according to strict rules about the use of PESTICIDES and ADDITIVES, ANIMAL WELFARE and SUSTAINABILITY. As more consumers become aware of their health and the state of their environment, sales of organic food have increased.

The ethical consumer realises that the production of organic foods is less damaging to the environment than conventional farming, as it causes less pollution from chemicals, is less harmful to wildlife and contributes less to global warming and climate change.

Producing food organically can involve more time and effort than conventional farming. Animals farmed organically for their meat often grow more slowly, so farmers have to wait longer before their livestock can be sold. These factors help to explain why organic food costs more than conventionally produced food.

Fairtrade

® Some products carry the FAIRTRADE Mark like the one on the left. It means that the people who supplied the raw materials for the products – such as cotton for clothing or cocoa beans for chocolate – have been paid a fair price. Fairtrade ensures that producers in developing countries get a better deal.

Look for the Fairtrade Mark on products
www.fairtrade.org.uk

This table shows the growth in the value of sales of Fairtrade products since 1998.

Retail value of sales of Fairtrade products in the UK (£ million)								
	1998	1999	2000	2001	2002	2003	2004	2005
Coffee	13.7	15.0	15.5	18.6	23.1	34.3	49.3	65.8
Tea	2.0	4.5	5.1	5.9	7.2	9.5	12.9	16.6
Chocolate/cocoa	1.0	2.3	3.6	6.0	7.0	10.9	16.5	21.9
Honey products	n/a	> 0.1	0.9	3.2	4.9	6.1	3.4	3.5
Bananas	n/a	n/a	7.8	14.6	17.3	24.3	30.6	47.7
Other	n/a	n/a	n/a	2.2	3.5	7.2	27.3	39.5
TOTAL	**16.7**	**21.8**	**32.9**	**50.5**	**63.0**	**92.3**	**140.0**	**195.0**

Adapted from www.fairtrade.org.uk

 Activity 4

Use the information in the table above to answer the following questions.

a) Which Fairtrade product was most popular in 2005?

b) What was the retail value (in millions) of tea sold in 1998?

c) The retail value of coffee in 2001 was £18.6 million. Round this to the nearest whole number.

d) In 2005, £39.5 million worth of other Fairtrade products were sold in the UK. What products might this include?

e) What was the percentage increase in the retail value of bananas between 2004 and 2005?

f) The retail value of coffee increased by 33 per cent between 2004 and 2005. Assuming the same increase each year, what will be the retail value of coffee in 2007?

g) When rounded to the nearest million pounds the retail values in 2001 were:

Coffee	19 million
Tea	6 million
Chocolate/cocoa	6 million
Honey products	3 million
Bananas	15 million
Other	2 million

Illustrate this data on a pie chart.

Animal Testing

Many products have been tested on animals before we buy them. Some cosmetics, toiletries and medicines are tested to ensure that they are safe for humans to use. Animal testing often causes harm and suffering to the animals involved. An ethical consumer would find this unacceptable and would choose to buy products that have not been tested on animals. Such products will clearly state this on the label, which makes it easier for the consumer to make an informed choice.

 Activity 5

Organise a class debate on the following statement: 'Animal testing is never acceptable'.

Take into account the views expressed during the debate. Write down your personal feelings and opinions on this issue and draw your own conclusions.

'WHAT A LOAD OF RUBBISH' ... OR IS IT?

Reuse bags or buy a 'bag for life'. Supermarkets often offer recycling facilities for plastic bags.

Pass on magazines you have read to a friend or give them to your local health centre or dentist's surgery.

Buy products that carry the recycling logo and recycle all cardboard and paper.

Recycling aluminum cans saves a lot of energy.

Buy loose fruit and vegetables if possible or look for BIODEGRADABLE trays if you buy pre-packed.

If possible buy large packs to reduce packaging waste.

Most rubbish in Northern Ireland is buried in landfill sites. This can become a major problem, as gases produced by the waste contribute to global warming, water supplies can become contaminated, and the sites attract pests such as rats. Eventually areas available for landfill sites in Northern Ireland will run out. Recycling is one way of reducing the amount of waste sent to landfill sites and there are many ways in which an ethical consumer can contribute to recycling.

 ## Activity 6

Carry out a survey to find out attitudes towards recycling. You might want to ask people what they recycle, why they recycle and how they do it. Write a report of your findings.

 ## Activity 7

In groups select one of the issues discussed in this chapter to use as a focus for an awareness-raising campaign in your school. You could include some of the following ideas:

- posters
- leaflets
- PowerPoint presentation
- flyers
- badges
- webpage
- newsletter
- article for school magazine.

REVIEW

 a) Take time to examine and read the information in the campaign produced by another group in the class for Activity 7. Get together and discuss your views and opinions on each other's work. Talk about the strengths of the campaign and any ways you feel they could improve.

b) Complete the following:
- Three things I learned through this chapter are ...
- Two things I enjoyed about this chapter are ...
- One thing I would still like to find out about is ...

c) Draw up a list of keywords relevant to this topic.

Activity 1

Carry out a class survey to find out how many people have shopped online. Find out the types of products bought, the most popular websites in your class and the methods of payment used. Present your findings.

Learning intentions

I am learning:

- ✓ how online shops try to influence consumer choices and decisions
- ✓ the advantages and disadvantages of shopping online
- ✓ to experiment with different designs and ideas in order to create a website homepage
- ✓ how the Consumer Protection (Distance Selling) Regulations 2000 protect me when I shop online.

The way we shop has changed dramatically and many people now shop online from the comfort of their own home. Shopping online is really using an online catalogue – you look through the lists and possibly photographs of all the items for sale, choose the products you like and send off your order. Most online shops use the shopping basket method. You tour the site and click on an item that you want to buy. The item will then be placed into a virtual shopping basket. When it's time to pay you register and are taken to a secure part of the shopping site where you give details of your credit or debit card. If the seller is satisfied with your payment details, your order will be placed and items will be delivered to the address you have given.

RETAILERS give a lot of attention to the design and layout of their website as consumers will be greatly influenced when choosing where to shop by the design and quality of the site. The homepage is like a shop window, used to attract consumers in, and it should be attractive and eye-catching.

 ## Activity 2

Visit two internet shopping sites such as www.tesco.com and www.sainsburys.co.uk or www.amazon.co.uk and www.waterstones.com. Use the following questions to help you compare the sites and decide which one you feel is the best. You can also develop your own questions to compare the sites.

a) Which site is easier to open and access?
b) Which site is easier to browse?
c) Which site design is more appealing and why?
d) Which site offers the best view of the items?
e) What strategies have been used by the online shops to encourage consumers to buy?
f) Which site offers the best delivery option?
g) What methods of payment can be used?

Present your findings as a report produced using ICT.

Many people now shop online.

Advantages of shopping online

Price – As staff costs are much lower than in a high street store, shopping online means that many items can be bought more cheaply.
Choice – It is possible to visit online shops from all around the world meaning that the choice of products available is much greater.
Convenience – You are able to shop at a time that suits you from any computer. This is good for people who live far from shops and for times when it is difficult to get to the shops e.g. when there is a new baby in the home, sickness or a busy lifestyle.
Delivery – Most internet shops deliver products within a few days to the doorstep.

Disadvantages of shopping online

Delivery – Delivery times vary and you might have to wait some time for your items. Also, delivery may only be during working hours, which is inconvenient for some people.
Quality – It is harder to judge the quality of the item you are buying until it is delivered.
Costs of delivery and return – Many online shops charge for delivery and if the item is unsuitable it has to be returned, which may also cost extra money.
Costs of shopping online – Although the cost of using the internet is getting cheaper, many internet providers still charge per minute. Browsing on the shopping sites can take some time and therefore could cost quite a lot of money.
Impulse buying – It is easy to get carried away and overspend when shopping online as everything is available at a click of the mouse. This overspending can lead to debt.

 ## Activity 3

Plan and create a homepage for a new supermarket. Remember to use the homepage as the shop window to the site. Include information that would attract consumers and make them want to shop there.

FAQs ABOUT SHOPPING ONLINE

Q

How can I be sure my details are safe and won't be accessed by others when I pay for items online?

A

You are advised to shop from well-known sites on the internet and from those that have secure payment procedures. These procedures ensure that before you give your credit or debit details you are moved to a secure part of the site. You can check that this has happened by ensuring that there is a padlock sign at the bottom of your screen. If a credit card is fraudulently used the consumer can cancel the contract and get a refund of any money paid from the card company. There are very few reports of card fraud from well-known sites.

Q

I've heard of PayPal but I'm not sure exactly what it is.

A

PayPal is a company that allows anyone who has an email address to send and receive payments online. PayPal is available in 55 countries and has more than 100 million customer accounts worldwide. This method of payment is safe, easy and quick to use.

Q

What are internet auction sites and how do they work?

A

Internet auction sites have become a very popular way to shop. eBay is one of the most widely used auction sites with a wide range of items sold on the site. Sellers can advertise their unwanted goods and if you want to buy something from the site you can place a bid. The person with the highest bid will then get the opportunity to purchase that item.

Q

What are my consumer rights when shopping online?

A

Consumers are protected when shopping online by the Consumer Protection (Distance Selling) Regulations 2000. These regulations give consumers rights when they shop via the internet, TV or telephone, or from a catalogue or magazine. Consumers are entitled to:

- clear information – before they order – about the supplier's name/address, cost of the goods, delivery costs and arrangements, how to pay and how to cancel
- cancel an order within seven working days (the first day being the day after you receive the goods)
- a full refund if the goods or services are not delivered within 30 days. Certain items such as perishable goods like flowers and fresh food and personalised goods cannot be returned.

Q

What if I order and pay for an item and it is never delivered to me?

A

The Distance Selling Regulations state that consumers should receive delivery of their item, unless otherwise agreed, within 30 days of placing the order. If the items do not arrive you can cancel the order and get your money back.

REVIEW

a) Choose a partner and take turns to read each other's homepage from Activity 3. Tell each other about the strengths of the homepage and suggest any improvements you feel they could make.

b) Decide together what makes a good homepage. Here are some ideas that may help you:
- colourful pictures or photographs of products on sale
- eye-catching use of lettering and colour
- slogans and logos
- well-organised, easy-to-read information.

How do your homepages match the suggestions above?

c) How would you improve on your work?

HOW ARE YOU PAYING?

Learning intentions

I am learning:

- ✓ how debit and credit cards are used to pay for goods and services
- ✓ about other methods of paying for goods and services
- ✓ how debt affects people's lives and how to avoid getting into debt
- ✓ to record information.

PAYING WITH CARDS

There are various ways to pay for goods and services. As well as paying by cash, many consumers now use debit and credit cards. Debit and credit cards are used to pay when shopping online.

Debit Cards

Maestro is the internationally recognised name for debit cards. Maestro can be used at seven million outlets in over 100 countries including withdrawing cash from Automated Telling Machines (ATM). When a consumer pays using a debit card the amount

The Maestro logo is used on debit cards.

of money spent is automatically taken from their bank account by Electronic Funds Transfer. As the money is taken directly from the bank account there is no bill at the end of the month. It is therefore easy to see what has been spent and how much money is left, and so avoid getting into debt.

Credit Cards

Many banks, finance companies and retailers supply credit cards. Consumers apply to a company for a credit card and must meet certain criteria set by the company. If a credit card is issued, the card company will set a CREDIT LIMIT. This must not be exceeded. The consumer can then use the credit card to pay for goods and services. The credit card company pays the retailer and sends a monthly statement to the consumer stating how much is owed. The consumer then pays the card company. INTEREST is charged if the total amount on the statement is not paid in full. This means that the initial amount of money owed will greatly increase when interest is added on. It is very easy to overspend using a credit card and many people find themselves in debt, unable to pay back the amount owed.

Credit cards are a way of borrowing money.

Chip and PIN

When using debit and credit cards, consumers are asked to enter a four-digit number into an electronic keypad. This number is known as a Personal Identification Number (PIN). Each cardholder has their own unique number and it is important not to tell anyone else what your PIN is, to prevent the card being used without your knowledge. Each individual card has a microchip carrying all the consumer's bank details.

Chip and **PIN**

The chip and PIN symbol.

DEBT

A consumer is in debt if their spending exceeds their ability to pay. They may be charged high interest rates if they are not able to pay the amount they owe on credit cards and this creates an even bigger problem. Some consumers borrow from many different providers and may have a mortgage, car loans, personal loans, store cards, and catalogue accounts as well as credit cards.

People's lives are greatly affected by debt and being in debt has many consequences for individuals and families.

 Activity 1

Discuss and make a list of the advantages and disadvantages of paying by cash, by debit card and by credit card.

 Activity 2

The cartoon below shows some tips for avoiding debt. Which three pieces of advice do you think are most useful? Explain your choices.

REVIEW

a) Complete the following:
- Three things I learned through this chapter are ...
- Two things I enjoyed about this chapter are ...
- One thing I would still like to find out about is ...

b) Draw up a list of keywords relevant to this chapter.

88

Learning intentions

I am learning:

✓ about the rights I have as a consumer
✓ how to apply my consumer rights in a range of situations.

18 facts that will make you a clever consumer!

1. If you change your mind about something you've bought, you are not automatically entitled to a refund.

2. Many retailers offer refunds on unwanted goods as a goodwill gesture to keep customers happy and willing to shop there again.

3. Knowing your rights means you can complain effectively when something is not up to scratch.

4. The Consumer Protection Act 1987 protects you by making it an offence for someone to sell goods that aren't safe.

5. Get what you pay for – the Weights and Measures (NI) Order 1981 makes it an offence to sell a short weight or measure.

6. Goods you buy should always be exactly as they are described – a waterproof coat should be waterproof and keep you dry.

7. If you feel that you have bought a product that is not the correct weight or measure, you can contact the Trading Standards Service. Inspectors regularly test weighing and measuring equipment.

8. Goods you buy should carry out the job you bought them for – in other words, they should be 'fit for the purpose'. For example, hair straighteners should straighten your hair.

9. Goods you buy should be of satisfactory quality – you expect a new product to be new, unused and working as it should.

10. If you are made aware of a fault in a product before you decide to buy, you will not be legally entitled to a refund or replacement if you change your mind.

11. Food labels provide information about the food you are buying – it's important to understand what they mean.

12. Food should be fit for consumption and free from contamination – any food outlet selling food that fails these requirements should be reported to Environmental Health.

13. Food outlets and food workers should maintain a high standard of hygiene and cleanliness and should be reported to Environmental Health if they don't.

14. It is a criminal offence to sell COUNTERFEIT GOODS, and buying them is supporting illegal trade.

15. Counterfeit goods may not meet required safety standards and could therefore be dangerous. This is not a wise way to spend your money.

16. Be aware of security when shopping online and only purchase from secure sites.

17. Comparing prices and looking out for special deals will ensure that your money is spent wisely.

18. Being an ethically aware consumer will provide more job opportunities for local people, support local business and help the environment.

Activity 1

James was given a new games console for his fourteenth birthday. After just six weeks it stopped playing the games. James and his mum returned to the shop where it was bought expecting a full refund or replacement. The young shop assistant was sympathetic but said there was nothing she could do.

a) Read the eighteen facts opposite. Which ones would be of use to James and his mum? What advice would you give them?

b) Decide on a way James could complain about this issue. He could write a letter, e-mail or return to the shop to speak to the manager. Write or role-play his complaint.

CONSUMER LEGISLATION

There are several laws that protect consumers in situations where they spend their money and things go wrong.

Weights and Measures (Northern Ireland) Order 1981

This Order controls the trade use of weighing and measuring equipment and sets out how goods should be sold by weight or measure.

The Sale and Supply of Goods Act 1994

Under the Act you can expect that any goods you buy are entitled to be:

- of satisfactory quality
- fit for any particular purpose made known to the seller; and
- as described.

Trade Descriptions Act 1968

Under the Trade Descriptions Act 1968, it is a criminal offence for a trader to make false statements about goods offered for sale.

Consumer Protection (Northern Ireland) Order 1987

Part III of this order makes it a criminal offence for a trader to give consumers a misleading indication about the price of any goods, services, accommodation or facilities, e.g. a shelf edge label or price list shows the price of the goods as £1.50 but the customer is charged £1.80 at the till, or an advertisement does not mention that the customer has to pay delivery charges.

 Activity 2

Look at each of the scenarios below and identify which law on page 89 will protect the consumer in each situation. Explain your answers.

REVIEW

 Explain to the class:
a) three facts you have learned about your consumer rights
b) two things you found difficult about this chapter
c) one question you still have about your consumer rights.

My train is always late. I wonder who I can speak to.

I would like help with sorting out my credit card debt.

Learning intentions

I am learning:

✓ about the different CONSUMER ORGANISATIONS that could help in a range of situations
✓ to adapt my behaviour and language appropriately for a task
✓ to respect the views and opinions of others and use negotiation and compromise when working as a group.

The DVD I bought in the market has damaged my DVD player. I think it was fake. Who can I report it to?

I found a piece of glass in my Chinese meal last night – who I shall report it to?

My friend gets *Which?* magazine sent to her house. What's that all about?

A number of organisations have been set up to help people with a range of consumer problems. Many problems that consumers experience can be resolved; however, it is sometimes difficult to find out who can help you in a range of situations.

 ## Activity 1

Use the information in the table on page 92 to find out who can help each of the consumers above with their problem.

Who are they?	How can they help consumers?	How can I get in touch with them?
Citizens Advice Bureau (CAB)	The CAB is the largest advice charity in Northern Ireland. Its offices can be found in many large towns. It offers advice on a wide range of issues such as: • debt problems • housing issues • consumer problems • employment issues. Its service is free of charge and is confidential.	www.citizensadvice.co.uk www.adviceguide.org.uk
General Consumer Council for Northern Ireland (GCCNI) The Consumer Council	The Consumer Council is an independent consumer organisation working to bring about change that will benefit Northern Ireland consumers. The Consumer Council handles complaints about: • planes, trains, buses, ferries • natural gas, electricity or coal.	www.consumercouncil.org.uk www.gccni.org.uk www.consumerline.org
Trading Standards Service Department of Enterprise, Trade and Investment www.detini.gov.uk	Trading Standards Service (TSS) seeks to protect the public in Northern Ireland by inspecting trade/business premises to ensure they comply with a wide range of consumer protection legislation. The laws, protecting consumers, include those relating to descriptions applied to goods or services; misleading price indications; the sale of counterfeit goods; the accuracy of weighing or measuring instruments and the quantity of goods sold. TSS provides advice to businesses and manages ConsumerLine, the telephone helpline for consumers.	www.tradingstandards.detini.gov.uk
Environmental Health Department	The Environmental Health Department is responsible for enforcing health and safety legislation in relation to food. Environmental Health inspectors can inspect any food premises at any time to ensure that the food or drink being served is safe and fit for consumption.	Contact the Environmental Health Department of the local district council.
Which? which?	Which? is the UK's largest independent consumer organisation. The Which? magazines it produces aim to provide consumers with useful information on a range of products. The organisation conducts independent tests on these products and recommends which product would be the 'Best Buy'.	www.which.co.uk

Activity 2

Find out more about one of the consumer organisations listed on page 92. Create a poster to make the public more aware of this organisation and how it can help consumers.

CONSUMER PROGRAMMES

There are also some consumer programmes on television and radio, such as BBC's *Watchdog*. Their aim is to help consumers by highlighting problems that they have experienced, confronting manufacturers and service providers, and giving advice about the best course of action.

Watchdog is a popular programme which deals with consumer issues.

 Activity 3

The producer of a new television programme dealing with teenagers' consumer problems has asked you to plan and create a lively and informative television show.

a) In groups, plan the content of one programme lasting no longer than ten minutes. You will need to consider the following in your planning and decision-making:
- the topic of the week
- the name of your show
- the format of your show
- who your guests will be
- how you will make sure your programme appeals to the teenage audience
- the role that each member of your group will play, including show host, guests, audience and director.

b) Put on a performance of your programme.

REVIEW

In your group, watch the other groups perform their programme from Activity 3. Write down two things your group liked about their work and think of one way they could enhance their programme.

GLOSSARY

Additives chemicals added to foods to improve their colour, flavour or appearance.

Anaemia a condition caused by a lack of iron in the body; the symptoms include looking pale and feeling weak.

Animal testing testing products such as cosmetics, toiletries and medicines on animals, to ensure that they are safe for humans to use.

Animal welfare ensuring that animals raised for food are well cared for, in a way that shows consideration for their natural behaviour.

Antibodies substances produced by certain cells in the body to fight infection.

Anti-oxidant vitamin vitamins A, C and E may offer some protection against coronary heart disease and some cancers by preventing substances in the body called free radicals from damaging arteries and the cells that repair such damage.

Bacteria microscopic organisms, some of which can cause disease (singular: bacterium).

Balance of Good Health a commonly used way of dividing foods into five food groups, all of which are needed for good health.

Balanced diet a range of foods from each of the five food groups in the correct proportions.

Beri-beri a disease that occurs when the body is deficient in vitamin B1, which affects the nervous system, digestive system and heart.

Best before date food will be at its best up until this date. Most foods with this type of date mark are low-risk foods and can be stored in a cupboard.

Biodegradable able to decay and break down naturally into harmless substances.

Budget a plan that shows how much money is available and how much is needed to pay for essential expenses and other spending.

Calcium a mineral found in dairy products that is essential for the growth and repair of bones and teeth.

Campylobacter a bacterium found in the intestines of many animals, which can lead to food poisoning. It can infect humans through contact with raw poultry, meat and unpasteurised milk.

Carbohydrate a nutrient needed for energy in the form of starch and sugar.

Cholesterol a fatty substance that can clog the arteries.

Clostridium botulinum a very rare form of food poisoning that can be fatal. It may result from eating damaged tinned food, especially meat and vegetables.

Consumer a person who buys or uses goods or services.

Consumer organisations help consumers to deal with problems such as poor service or the failure of retailers to comply with the law.

Contamination occurs when something gets into food that should not be there, for example, bacteria, a hair, or a fly. This will affect the quality of the food and can cause food poisoning.

Cook-chilled cooked by the manufacturer, then rapidly chilled and stored below 5°C.

Coronary heart disease can occur when the small arteries that supply blood to the heart become blocked by a build-up of fatty deposits.

Counterfeit goods goods that appear to be a well-known brand but are actually fakes.

Credit limit the maximum amount of money that can be borrowed using a credit card.

Danger zone the temperature at which bacteria multiply most readily, between 5°C and 63°C.

Deficiency shortage.

Dehydration a lack of water in the body.

Diabetes a condition in which the body's normal way of breaking down sugar is not functioning properly. This means the pancreas is not producing any or enough insulin to regulate the amount of sugar (glucose) in the blood.

E coli A food poisoning bacterium that is very dangerous for pregnant women, the very young and the elderly. It can be found on raw and undercooked meats, unpasteurised milk and dairy foods.

Emotional needs our need to feel, for example, happy, content, loved and secure.

Ethical relating to morals and values. An ethical consumer is one who considers issues such as low pay for farmers or animal welfare when they choose goods and services.

Extended family a type of family structure that includes parents, grandparents, aunts, uncles and cousins, who may live together or nearby.

Fairtrade a guarantee that a fair price has been paid to the farmer for his produce.

Fibre substances in food that are not digested but are important to help remove waste from the body.

Folic acid a vitamin supplement which, when taken up to the twelfth week of pregnancy, can reduce the risk of spina bifida and other neural tube defects in the unborn baby.

Food hygiene ensuring that food is safe to eat and has been protected from contamination.

Food miles the measure of the distance a food travels from field to plate.

Food poisoning an illness that can occur 1–36 hours after eating contaminated food. Symptoms may include vomiting, diarrhoea, nausea, abdominal pain and fever.

Fortified containing nutrients that have been added to improve the food's nutritional value.

Foster family a family structure in which children are cared for by foster parents because their natural parents are unable to look after them.

Function role, job.

Haemoglobin the red oxygen-carrying pigment in red blood cells.

Halal food that Muslims are permitted to eat, according to their religion. Vegetables, fruit, grain and seafood are halal, and so is meat (except pork) if the animal has been killed in the correct way.

Hormones chemicals produced naturally by the body and carried in the blood. Each hormone performs a different role in the body.

Immune system processes in the body that protect it against infection.

Income Money received, from wages, state benefits, pocket money.

Intellectual needs our need for things to keep our brain active, such as education, books and play.

Interest a charge made for borrowing money, usually a percentage of the amount borrowed.

Kwashiorkor a disease caused by a lack of protein in the diet.

Life cycle the stages we go through during our life.
Listeria a food poisoning bacterium which can be particularly harmful to pregnant women and can lead to miscarriage and stillbirth. It can be found in soft cheeses, pâté, meat, milk products, prepared salads and cook-chilled foods.

Manufacturer a maker of goods.
Meat alternatives high-protein food products that can be eaten as an alternative to meat, e.g. soya, Quorn, texturised vegetable protein (TVP) and tofu.
Menopause when periods stop and natural fertility ends, usually between the ages of 45 and 55.
Minerals substances such as calcium, iron and fluoride that are needed in minute quantities by the body for a variety of functions.
Mortgage money borrowed from a bank or building society to buy a house.
Mutual respect when people show consideration for each other.

Nuclear family a family structure that includes parents and their children, living together.
Nutrients nutrients include carbohydrates, protein, fat, vitamins and minerals. These are chemicals found naturally in food that are essential for growth, development and functioning of the body.

Obesity a condition in which an individual is at least 20 per cent over the ideal weight for their height and build.
Organic produced according to strict rules about the use of pesticides and additives, animal welfare and sustainability.
Osteomalacia a disease that occurs when the body is deficient in vitamin D. This disease causes weak bones in adults.
Osteoporosis a condition in which the bones become weak and brittle, and break easily.

Pellagra a disease that occurs when the body is deficient in the B vitamin niacin. It is marked by shrivelled skin, wasted body, mental illness and paralysis.

Personal hygiene making sure the body is clean. This is important for food preparation in order to prevent food poisoning.
Pesticides chemicals used to kill insect pests that attack crops.
Physical needs food, water and warmth, the basic requirements that we need to stay alive and healthy.
Polyunsaturated fats fats containing no cholesterol.
Probiotic a feature of some yoghurts and yoghurt drinks. Some research has shown that probiotic foods may help to promote a healthy digestive system and improve the immune system.
Protein a nutrient needed for growth, repair and maintenance of the body.

Ramadan the ninth month of the Muslim year, when Muslims do not eat or drink between sunrise and sunset.
Rent a regular payment made for the use of a house that is owned by another person.
Retailer a shop, or anyone who sells goods directly to consumers.
Rickets a disease that occurs in children when the body is deficient in vitamin D, causing bones to bend.
Role reversal occurs when traditional male and female gender roles within the home are reversed.

Salmonella a bacterium found in the intestines of many animals which can lead to food poisoning. It can be found in poultry, sausage, eggs and raw meat.
Saturated fat a type of fat found in animal foods that can contribute to the blocking of arteries. This may result in coronary heart disease.
Scurvy a disease that occurs when the body is deficient in vitamin C.
Service something that consumers can pay for in order to help them in some way, e.g. hairdressing, a taxi service.
Shared roles occurs when family members work together in the home.
Single-parent family a family structure in which one parent has sole responsibility for the upbringing of their child.
Social needs the need to be in contact with others and be accepted by others.
Source a food that contains a particular nutrient.

Staphylococcus aureus a food poisoning bacterium, which may be found in cooked meat, pies, custard. It can also be transferred to food from the nose, skin, infected cuts and boils.
Stepfamily a family structure that occurs when two adults with children from a previous relationship get married.
Supplements tablets, drops or medicine taken to add minerals and vitamins to the diet.
Sustainability using resources in such a way that they are not completely destroyed or used up.

Toxoplasmosis a tiny parasite that can cause blindness or brain damage in an unborn baby. It is found in unpasteurised milk, products made from it and raw or undercooked meats.
Unpasteurised milk milk that has not been treated by heating to kill germs.
Use by date this means that food must be eaten by this date. After this date food is likely to become unsafe to eat and could cause food poisoning.

Vacuum packaging packaging from which air has been removed, which means that the food inside stays fresh longer.
Vitamins substances that are present in various foods and are essential, in tiny amounts, to keep people healthy.

Weaning gradually changing from a diet of only milk to a variety of foods.

INDEX